It's Okay, Señora

My family lands in Colombia's drug war

This book is a work of non-fiction. Names of Colombians have been changed to guard identity. All other names are true to life.

Dorothy Siebert

Published by Señora Publishing, December, 2020
ISBN: 9781777439408

Typeset: Greg Salisbury
Book Cover Design: Greg Salisbury

TABLE OF CONTENTS

PART I
August 1989

PART II
August 1987 - August 1989

PART III
August 1989

Wednesday, August 30, 1989. That night a miracle happened in Medellín—complete silence. The *toque de queda* took effect.

No people crowded the sidewalks, no buses rattled through the streets, no cars honked. The myriad vendors and beggars disappeared. Even our pedalling watchman with his bicycle bell stayed home. A heavy waiting fell over the city.

Three million silent people.

Just before ten o'clock I heard gunshots.

I ran upstairs, then through the gray light of the boys' bedroom where they slept in their bunk beds. As quietly as I could I slipped the bolt on the steel door and stepped onto the little balcony that faced the street.

But I saw nothing. The street was empty. Every house shut tight.

Who had fired? At whom and why? Had someone broken curfew in the next street? No commotion followed, only that eerie silence. No answers.

It came to me how Karen Blixen had written in *Out of Africa* that a single shot in the night felt strangely as though someone had cried out a message in one word and would not repeat it.

I stood, straining against the metal railing. It was so silent that for the first time in our two years there, I heard the church bells from the next barrio ringing on the hour. Were they calling in vain for the faithful to come to late mass?

Or maybe they sang out, "Fear not—all shall be well."

———————————————

PART I
AUGUST 1989

In Winnipeg, before flying back to Medellín, August 1989: Andrew, Conrad, Harold, Dorothy, Matthew, Rebecca. Photo by Wally Schmidt.

1   A Pablo Escobar welcome

Friday, August 18, 1989. On that drizzly, dark August day at 5 a.m., we stood in line at the Winnipeg airport. Furlough in our home country, Canada, was over. I fumbled sleepily to fill out the customs forms. No breakfast yet. I already missed Cheerios. Three years would be a long wait without them. Our tickets, stapled together, showed the cities of our flight changes: Winnipeg-Minneapolis-Miami-Medellín.

The first indication of something suspicious was the pilot announcing mid-flight an unscheduled stop between Miami and Medellín, on San Andres Island. No engine trouble was cited and the Colombian passengers remained surprisingly calm.

We were ordered to stay seated. A slim woman in uniform entered and marched to the back of the plane followed by a stout, disheveled man in a wrinkled tourist shirt. A disguise. He moved purposefully to the rear of the plane from where he proceeded slowly forward, questioning each male passenger in turn.

"Your point of origin? Your passport. Your identity card."

Tense silence filled the cabin but no information was given out. What was it all about we whispered to each other.

We were soon back in the air approaching José Maria Cordova Airport, its beautiful glass dome like a diamond set amid the dark blue mountains around Medellín. I brushed the unscheduled stop out of my mind as a security annoyance, much like the military roadblocks we were used to throughout Medellín.

Our family was made up of Harold and me plus our four children. Matthew was 14, Rebecca 11, Andrew 8 and Conrad 5. Each of their backpacks and our mismatched suitcases was stuffed with treasures from Canada. Shells picked up on the West Coast. Posters of Arctic wolves. English books. Dozens of pins of the Canadian flag to give our Colombian friends. And in a blue canvas hockey bag, so handy for bulky objects, I'd packed special baking pans and sweaters with motifs of loons and cabins in the wild.

It would be late when we got to our house in Medellín. The kids would need to get to bed.

But not before I checked their beds for glass shards.

Chapter 1

"A bomb blew up at your house," our co-worker, Galen Wiest, had called to tell us while we were in Winnipeg on furlough. "All your front windows were blown out. The garage door, too. The front of your neighbour's house that touches yours was sheared away. About five other houses were affected, too."

The news had shocked our parents more than us. Two years working in Medellín had inured us to news of violence. And we were pretty sure where the bomb came from. Retaliation for one of Harold's wilder moments, chasing down thieves and getting them arrested.

"It was really fortunate," Galen went on to say, "that no one was hurt. Maria was watching our three kids at your house and we'd picked them up just minutes before this. If the kids had been there, man, I don't know...."

He went on, "The bunk beds and toy shelves are covered with glass shards."

We told the kids sketchily about the bomb, not the glass.

"You still want to go back to Medellín?" I asked them.

"Yes!" Andy had said. "I want to put up the posters I bought here!"

As the plane taxied to the gate, I squeezed Harold's hand and smiled down the row at our children.

"Almost home!" I said. Then a Simon and Garfunkel song drifted to my mind. *Homeward bound, I wish I was homeward bound.*

I was leaving home and going home, yet neither felt like home.

When we landed, the immigration officials hurriedly stamped all six passports and practically pushed us through customs. What a surprise! Immigration and customs were normally stringent. Why were they acting so oddly?

The sharp mountain air greeted us outside the airport. At this elevation, almost an hour's drive above Medellín, the air was crisp and cool and clean. Heavily armed soldiers in battle fatigues stood guard outside the airport but we paid them little attention. We happily embraced Galen and another co-worker, Peter Loewen, who had come to drive us home.

Peter, a tall, no-nonsense Canadian, saw us being waved through all the usual obstacles. "What a miracle!" he said. "They let you through without question and without opening a single bag. That's never happened in the more than twenty years we've been here."

The big blue hockey bag was squeezed into Peter's sturdy Nissan jeep along with Harold and our three eldest kids. I put the lighter bags into the back seat of Galen's tiny old Renault. I settled into the passenger seat and pulled sleepy Conrad onto my lap. No seatbelts yet in Colombia. I could feel the bumps on the road through the floorboards of that car but Galen himself was a reassuring presence, a team member we could count on to lessen tensions with his sense of humour.

Blackness enveloped us as the car turned onto the narrow road winding down the mountain. I peppered Galen with questions. How had the Colombians in our little Mennonite Brethren church fared during the past few months? All safe? No more guerrilla invasions in their barrio?

Suddenly our headlights picked out a uniformed soldier. He stood guard on the dirt shoulder in army fatigues, holding, at the ready, a semi-automatic rifle. Less than a hundred metres further down the mountain we passed another one, then others spaced the same distance apart.

"All these soldiers," Galen said. "Haven't seen that on this road before. Something's going on."

"Was there trouble today?" I asked.

"Don't know. Left home before the 6:30 news."

Soon we rounded a curve and a sea of lights swam into view.

Medellín is beautiful at night. The city, at an altitude of five thousand feet, fills a narrow valley encircled by the Andes Mountains. The barrios have inched their way up the sides of the mountains so that as high and as far as I could see it looked like the stars of heaven had dropped down over this troubled city. Even the wretched shantytowns were transformed into myriad specks of pure light.

The wealthy sector where drug lord Pablo Escobar lived looked as innocent as a baptismal font. The havoc he started that day, though, would change Colombia and would change our lives.

 2   Is there glass in the bunk beds?

Nearing the city, I felt a wave of claustrophobia, like I was walking into a cage. Besides the fear of guerrilla attacks and the threat of kidnapping, there was the ongoing violence by paramilitary groups and vigilantes. Then the daily killings by assassins hired by drug lords or the mafia to get rid of unwanted persons.

Amid the unrest, common criminals flourished. Everyone was on their guard at all hours. Don't get kidnapped. Don't get shot at. Don't wear jewellery on the bus. Don't carry a purse on the street. Don't go home alone after taking money from the bank. Don't let your child out of your sight.

The Renault and Nissan pulled up in front of our rented house and we piled out. The kids pushed forward, eager to get to their rooms.

Stepping into the house I was hit by that spectral sense one has after a long absence from a familiar place. The *sala* looked smaller than I remembered. And, after the wall-to-wall carpets in Canadian homes, the concrete tile felt cold and naked under my feet.

While the men unloaded the luggage, I stood in the front room, my eyes roving the windows and walls for bomb damage.

The rows of glass that made up the garage door and our entrance door had all been replaced with thick tempered glass. But between the glass sections the metal bars were now bent slightly out of line.

In the *sala* the large front window had been shattered. All the glass in its five tall sections had been replaced, the caulking fresh and clean.

I sighed and shook my head. Our wonderful co-workers, Galen and his wife Linda, had taken care of cleaning up and replacing everything in our absence. How could we ever thank them?

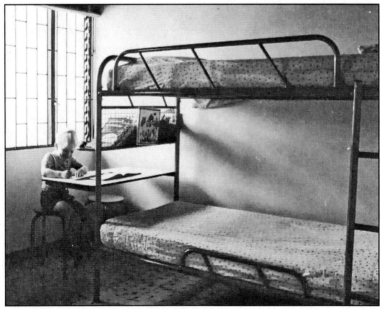

Conrad and the red bunk beds shortly after moving in, before we made the new quilts.

I walked up the open staircase of polished concrete to the second floor. On the landing I turned to look back at the living room. The cool night air breezed in through the bars at the open windows, billowing the linen drapes I'd sewn myself. It whispered, "You are home."

Yet I didn't feel quite at home. The bomb had intruded into our private space and the house now seemed a vulnerable place rather than a secure sanctuary.

Upstairs in Andy and Conrad's room, the red metal bunk beds stood as strong and sturdy as ever, though the paint was slightly chipped now. There was new glass in the window. It looked like all traces of a bomb blast had been scrupulously cleared away.

Were the beds all right? The bedding had been washed and rewashed.

I ran my hands over the pillows and under the bright quilts so cheerful with their boats, planes and trains in red, blue and yellow. I slid my hands between the quilts and the sheets. Nothing stung.

"Beds seem safe," I said to Harold. "Let's dig out pyjamas and get the boys ready for bed." While Harold rummaged in a suitcase, I looked over the red toy shelves that covered one wall, filled with cars and trucks, books, puzzles and games.

Things looked clean.

Then my eye fell on the Lego building blocks. Harold had built a low, wooden box on casters, two feet by four feet, to roll out of the way under the bottom bunk. The open box held thousands of pieces of Lego.

"Oh, no," I groaned. "Look at that."

Glints of light sparkled all over the box. Interlaced with the coloured blocks were tiny glass shards.

I groaned again. The boys stared.

Harold said, "No! Can't be." He bent down for a close look.

"Boys," he said, "no Lego. Do not touch the Lego! We'll clean all that up tomorrow." He shoved the box far under the bunk.

"Do we have to throw them all away?" asked Conrad.

"No dear." I kissed the boys' sweet faces, literally sweet with fruit drink stains from the plane ride. "Look at your faces! But I'm too tired to care. We'll wash that off tomorrow."

"I'll tuck them in and pray with them," Harold said, "You can unpack."

I paused in the hallway to breathe. This home felt less safe than I'd thought. Of course, there had been no notice in the papers about the bomb that damaged the houses on our street. And no police had come to investigate. Such incidents were minor in a country where the police force and the military were stretched thin, battling guerrilla armies and drug barons.

I opened Becky's door. Her room also faced the street and her large window had been shattered. But now the room looked as peaceful as a painting, with the wicker armoire holding her colourful ponies and a line of Beatrix Potter storybooks.

Becky perched on the edge of her bed, teasing her little dog, Mitzi, who was yelping with the excitement of having her home again. I ran my hands between the sheets and over the pink and white quilt on the double bed. The quilt was a gift lovingly hand-stitched by the women of our Mennonite Brethren church in Morden, Manitoba.

I gave her the all-clear and tucked her into bed. After the many different rooms we'd slept in over the past months, this girlie room felt reassuringly like home to me.

I said a prayer with her and we hugged. At the doorway I turned back.

"Are you okay here in your bed? You're not afraid if I turn off the light?"

She shook her head. "It's okay. Remember?" She pointed at a poster of Jesus in a robe, holding a lamb on his arm. That's right, I remembered. To fall asleep, she always looked at that poster my mother had sent. I let her keep Mitzi with her this first night home but, turning off the light, still felt a stab of apprehension.

The other two bedrooms, Matthew's and ours, faced the back courtyard. Their windows had stayed intact. In his room Matthew was filling shelves with the books he had dug up in used bookstores across Canada. He held up a book, *Quantum Physics*.

"Look Mom, I got this for fifty cents!"

I had no clue about the title but it was a thick book with a hard cover.

"Looks like fifty bucks!"

I gave him a big hug. I was grateful for our eldest son. He looked at Colombia as a grand adventure and the other kids followed his lead. Back in 1985 when the letter arrived in our little prairie town telling us of our mission assignment, we were thrilled. Matthew, then ten years old, snapped the letter from my hand and danced around the kitchen. "Yayy! We're going to Colombia! We're going to Colombia!"

I walked into the master bedroom next door. Assorted suitcases and a hockey bag were piled at the foot of our bed. Somewhere in there I had my own precious stash of books buried under clothing, baking pans and cake mixes. I quickly turned away and headed back downstairs. I loathe unpacking.

I heard Harold rummaging in the tiny study next to the kitchen, so I poured a cup of tea and sank down on the sand-coloured living room sofa. What a relief the three months of furlough, of travel and speaking engagements were behind us. Visiting churches and relatives from Ontario to British Columbia and down to Denver, Colorado, we had taken eighteen plane trips besides driving across the prairies.

"Thank God," I said aloud, "that was our last plane ride. I don't need to see an airport for a very long time. And no more hockey bags!"

My shoulders relaxed.

I didn't dream that in just two weeks' time I'd be on this same sofa, nerves taut and wracked with the pain of an impending decision. Do we dash for the airport or wait out the war?

 3   The drug war kicks off

The next morning, we pieced together what had happened the day of our flight back to Colombia. Luis Carlos Galán had been gunned down that day - August 18, 1989 - assassinated while addressing a rally. At forty-six years old, he was the much-favored candidate in the upcoming elections for president of Colombia. Admired for his stance against the drug traffickers, he brought a vibrancy, a vigour to the country—the people's hope for a happier future.

The drug lords hated him.

The El *Colombiano* newspaper reported that Galán had stood to speak on a high, makeshift platform before an enormous crowd. Shots rang out. In the panic and confusion, the assassins disappeared in the crowd. His death, the reporters wrote, no doubt ordered by drug lord Pablo Escobar.

In one sense it was no surprise. Political and judicial leaders in Colombia expected attacks. Kidnappings and massacres were a regular part of evening news. Any journalist brave enough to speak out against drug trafficking or corruption faced assassination threats.

More than eighty journalists had been assassinated in Colombia over the past decade.

But now Colombia said, Enough!

Within an hour of Galán's assassination, the Colombian president, Virgilio Barco Vargas spoke on national television. He ordered a crackdown on the drug lords by the police and the military as Colombia had never before seen.

Civil liberties were suspended.

Police searches could be made without warrants.

Suspects could be held for a week without charge.

He announced an executive decision—a previous extradition treaty with the United States was revived.

What did that mean?

It meant the drug barons, the mafia, could no longer hide out on their vast fincas, paying obscene bribes to be left alone. For them, Barco's announcement of extradition was an affront, an insult that called for all-out war. The ongoing, subdued drug war erupted into an all-out violent encounter between the narco-traffickers and the Colombian government.

The narco-traffickers were furious that members of their cartel were to be sent to the United States for trial and sentencing. They demanded a stop to extradition. The powerful Medellín drug cartel led by Escobar declared war against the government and against the people of Colombia.

For a few days Medellín seemed calm and quiet. An aura of anticipation hung over the streets, palpable like the breath of an eager guest outside the door.

Medellín nestled in the Andes Mountains.

Then war erupted. Bombings started.

Banks.

Stores.

Radio stations.

Political offices.

Travel agencies.

17 bombings in one week in our city alone.

Medellín's mayor begged the president of Colombia to send 3000 police reinforcements to Medellín. The papers reported that only 100 came.

In a statement on radio the drug lords declared a "total and absolute war" on the government, on judges, journalists and on anyone else who opposed them. We were shocked to read in the paper that the drug cartel had 4000 bombs ready to destroy "anything they want to" in order to weaken the country.

Everyone we talked with seemed terrified. Colombian families that could afford it started fleeing Medellín for other countries.

Next, the narcos lashed out against Americans. They threatened to kidnap or kill any Americans in Colombia: "We will not respect the families of those who have not respected our families!" The American embassy ordered all non-essential personnel out of the country.

Harold and I still felt safe though.

We were Canadian. Surely the drug lords would know the difference.

PART II
AUGUST 1987 - AUGUST 1989

Ready to take on anything. Morden, Manitoba. Conrad, Becky, Matthew, Harold, Andy, and me. Photo by Nikkel Photography

 ## 4   Let's just get on a bus and see

When we were first assigned to Colombia, my parents worried for us, "You'll be breathing the same air as Pablo Escobar!"

Medellín was his hometown and his base of operations. He was known to ruthlessly kill those who got in his way and he used the guerrilla groups for bombings and massacres, putting pressure on the government across whole regions of the country.

Colombia was an interesting place for a pacifist Mennonite. Peace was continually threatened by armed conflicts. In 1987, while we had waited in Costa Rica for our visas to enter Colombia, the drug cartel had sent a retaliatory message to all embassies in Colombia. In their message the drug lords threatened to kill one hundred "soft targets," that is, foreigners.

The Canadian embassy passed this information on to us. It warned us that the Canadian government could not ensure our safety if we went ahead and moved to this volatile country.

But we were certain we'd been called to Colombia by God and felt sure we would have divine protection. Even if bad things happened, we would take whatever came as part of the divine plan for our lives.

Moving to Colombia with my Albertan husband created new challenges for our marriage. From the start Harold and I disagreed on what it meant to take a risk. What I called risky, Harold usually insisted was safe. Perfectly safe.

Harold and I had been married fifteen years when we moved to Colombia. His grandparents had been pioneers in northern Alberta, clearing land and living without modern amenities. Harold himself remembered when the telephone and electricity had reached his home. As a boy he had held the reins of horse-drawn sleds in winter and watched his father break in broncos. As the eldest child he had spent his boyhood outdoors driving tractor and caring for animals. My own youth had been a straight-laced town life and I saw Harold's background as intriguingly romantic.

Yet I hadn't recognized in him what our coworkers saw very soon.

Rambo! That's what they called him.

I can still see him standing there among our trunks and suitcases in 1987 on our first full day in Medellín. Unpacking was not on his mind.

"Let's just get on a bus," he said, "and see where we end up!"

"With the children?" I bleated.

"Of course!"

"But we don't have a map of the city. We don't even know where we are right now."

"It'll be perfect. I can find my way back here, no problem."

It was true that Harold was gifted with an innate sense of direction. Even in strange cities, he seemed to always know how to find his way through the most complex maze.

"Why don't you go on your own and check things out?" I said. "Then, later, we can all go together."

I said later but meant never.

Away he went to explore Medellín, a great gleam in his eye.

An hour later he showed up in the doorway, looking pale and disturbed. So unlike him. His bus, he explained, had been stopped by a crowd in a street. A man had been shot and killed a few blocks away.

Celebrating the day we bought the jeep

Harold whispered to me, "The man was lying there. Blood running down the sidewalk and into the street."

Then in a louder voice he announced to the kids in his usual short bursts of words, "Tomorrow I'm going out. Find a jeep. These steep streets. Just what the family needs."

The man killed on the street that day was a university professor. A conflict was going on at the Universidad de Medellín and many professors were assassinated. That fall the whole university was shut down and students lost an entire year of study.

When we'd been in Colombia for three months, the government declared "total war" against the armed groups causing havoc in the country: guerrilla armies, paramilitaries and drug traffickers. Although called "total war," that attempt to quell conflict did not lead to the level of violence that began in 1989 when we returned from furlough, but it did lead to many more assassinations and demonstrations.

The adventures we had during our first two years in Medellín caused our families back home to question our wisdom. But that did not dampen our commitment.

All four sets of Harold's and my grandparents had escaped the Russian Revolution of the 1920s, immigrating to Canada. They knew no English and arrived with little more than the clothes on their backs. Their stories of escape and survival infused us with compassion for suffering people and inspired us to embrace the adventure of mission work. We were young enough to believe we could handle anything, plus we felt sure we were exactly where we were meant to be.

🌹 5 Surprise!

By 1987, our branch of Mennonites had worked in Colombia for more than forty years. They had established churches in other regions of the country but in the city of Medellín they had only one church. It was in the barrio of Salvador.

Harold and I arrived as the first members of a new team being formed to work in that city. John Savoia, the Mennonite Brethren team leader drove up from Cali in his jeep to orient us. A wonderful, gentle man with rosy cheeks and a white beard, he found us a house to rent and introduced us to the church and its people.

As a child, the slide shows I'd seen at mission fests often showed the white missionary stepping down from the airplane into a sea of expectant faces. The natives, as we called them then, were more than thrilled, usually ecstatic, at the arrival of the foreign missionary.

Not so the Colombians.

On our second day in Medellín, John Savoia broke the news to us.

"You see, Colombians have never forgiven the States for taking Panama away from Colombia, so they don't take kindly to foreigners from the north."

Then he served us one more surprise.

"Your assignment's been changed, too. You were originally assigned to work alongside the Colombian pastor of the Medellín church. But, shortly before you arrived, the pastor, with his wife and children, up and suddenly moved to another city entirely. So now you are the pastor couple of the church. You'll be leading this church."

That sounded scary.

How equipped were we? We didn't know the culture. We had only one year of Spanish language instruction. We had little experience of big-city life.

Harold was 41 and I was 36. We had met at Bible College, married, had kids. Harold had degrees in theology and music and had been teaching at the Winkler Bible Institute, a Mennonite Brethren post-secondary school in southern Manitoba. I had a BA and teacher training but after Matthew was born I stopped teaching to follow my dreams as a writer while a stay-at-home mom. I had published about a dozen articles in religious and secular papers when I chose to give up my writing in favor of mission work, thinking that would please God more.

I had grown up a preacher's kid. My dad pastored churches and that seemed to me almost the highest calling. Missionary was THE highest. I was very pleased to see the pride my dad felt when Harold and I chose a mission assignment.

When in 1985 we were accepted for foreign mission work, we sold our belongings in a garage sale, rented out our house and drove from central Canada to Fresno, California with our four kids in a blue Volare station wagon pulling a compact trailer with our books and bedding. For one year we studied at the Mennonite Brethren Seminary to beef up our Bible knowledge and our understanding of current mission challenges. Then we returned to Manitoba, packed for overseas and moved to Costa Rica for a year of study at the Spanish Language Institute.

By the summer of 1987 we were ready to jump into the fray.

And a fray it was.

Not only was Medellín the homicide capital of the world at the time, the church we were assigned to was reeling from a scandal with a former missionary. Naturally the people were leery of a new set of missionaries. And we were the sole Mennonite Brethren missionaries in the city until reinforcements could arrive.

Our assignment was to build up this tiny, faltering church. In wake of the scandal, many had left, causing numbers to dwindle. We were to grow the number of members and bring new life to the flock.

That was the scene we stepped into—a small, disheartened band hanging on by their fingernails. I dreamed of re-igniting hope and of passing on to the people so much more than just the bland faith that the writer George Macdonald calls the passive acceptance of conventional opinion.

The church building itself was nothing to boast about. It was an unfinished construction. At the street level we saw a large concrete pad. Wide outdoor stairs led down to the basement where the meetings were held. The basement was built into the hillside, one side open to the elements and secured with a rolling gate of thick iron bars. The centre of the basement was an open meeting room with benches. Along one side of the room were three doorways hung with curtains leading to the Sunday School rooms.

At the back of the basement were two doors. One led to the only bathroom in the building and the other to the kitchen that was partitioned to include the bedroom of the married couple who lived in the church. A building could not be left empty and unguarded. So, this couple, also members of the church, guarded the church by living in it, poor as the proverbial church mice.

We tried to put our arms around what was left of the church, to rescue the fragments. Our aim was to help the people find hope through Jesus' teachings. The work challenged us in every way and we discovered reserves we never knew we had.

Entry to the church basement.

Our very first Sunday in Colombia, we met the church group that included several seniors, a few middle-aged men, a number of women, about eight young people and a scattering of children. They were cautious but received us kindly. All the adults shook our hands and I felt blessed by the women who hugged me.

After the morning service they held a welcoming lunch. From television shows they had learned that hot dogs were a popular part of the diet of North Americans so, wanting to please us, they served hot dogs for lunch.

The church pews made of wooden slats were moved around to face each other. I was shown to a bench in the centre along with our three youngest children. Harold and Matthew hung out with the men and youth standing around.

The church women handed each person a hot dog wrapped in a serviette. I looked down at mine. It was a dry bun holding a wiener topped with a sprinkle of crushed potato chips. Our three youngest children looked at me and I looked back at them with an encouraging smile. We had never before eaten naked hot dogs with no ketchup, no mustard, no relish.

All eyes were on us. The kids were good sports and besides, we were hungry. It tasted good! We smiled and nodded.

Drinks were handed out: coloured plastic tumblers half filled with *tinto*, hot, sugary black coffee. Every person was handed the same drink, from the oldest senior down to the smallest child. Our children then aged three to twelve took a sip of their drinks, looked at me again and then shyly set them down on the bench beside me.

I thought I'd better explain.

"I'm so sorry," I told the church women. "*Desculpe.* Our children have never tasted coffee before now."

The Colombians' eyes popped. Mouths dropped open.

"*Nunca?*"

"No, never."

"Well then, what did you put in their baby bottles?" asked a white-haired woman.

"Milk," I answered.

"Milk? Nothing more?"

"Just milk."

"Oh." The women looked around at each other and shook their heads. "*Que raro.* How odd."

An elderly woman whispered to another, "So *that's* why the children have such blonde hair."

"No, sister," answered a younger woman. "No, that's from genes, not milk."

6   Acclimatized yet?

Before arriving in Medèllín we had written the Mission Board with questions, one of which was, "How much time will we have to acclimatize to the changes before beginning work?" That turned out to be quite the joke. Our job started the first Sunday and just kept going.

"Acclimatized yet?" We teased each other after every startling incident and misunderstood conversation in our new setting.

Harold and I threw ourselves into the work. We could carry on a conversation in Spanish but, of course, our vocabulary was limited. Before we took our one year of study, we had not spoken any Spanish. We both knew German and that helped to understand another language. It was challenging to express complex ideas, though. Those first months, after conversations with other people, Harold and I would often turn to each other to say, "This is what I *think* they said. What do *you* think they said?"

I feel grateful to those church people. What patience they had with our limited language! How often they must have felt like laughing out loud at us but managed to suppress even the hint of a smile.

Two weeks after our arrival, still in a temporary suite waiting to move into our rental home, I found myself cooking a dinner for guests, three church members. It felt awkward as we had not unpacked our trunks and I had available only what was in the cupboards of the suite.

"I'm not ready for visitors, yet," I said to Harold. "Why did you invite them?"

"I don't remember inviting them. I was talking with the church elder saying we should meet together to discuss plans," Harold explained. "And suddenly he agreed they could come for dinner. I have no idea how it happened!"

Glitches in communication were part of getting used to a culture. I shook my head and wondered what Colombians would eat for supper.

I don't remember the rest of the meal but I sure remember that I served mashed potatoes. In Canada I had made mashed potatoes from any potatoes I happened to have in the house. Why would Colombian potatoes be any different?

The three guests came. Luis, church elder, cheerful and generous. Mariela his wife, thoughtful, a gentle soul. Valeria was with them, a high-energy leader among the youth. When the food was ready and hot and all I had left to do was mash the potatoes, I signalled to Harold to gather the kids and guests round the table.

In the kitchen I began with a hand masher. The potatoes were like a mass of glue. Maybe the electric mixer would do the trick? Still glue. More butter? More milk? No, a large, sticky mass of paste.

"I am so sorry," I said as I passed the mashed potatoes. "The Colombian potatoes are different from Canadian ones." I was confident our kids would not complain because I had made a strict rule in our home that there could be no grumbling about food during any meal since that would affect another person's ability to enjoy the meal. *After* a meal, they were free to say, "Yucky."

Our guests that day were too kind to criticize but I did learn from them that Colombia has dozens of varieties of potatoes and each one has its distinct characteristics. The next time I made mashed potatoes I chose the kind called Criolla. But that evening we smothered the paste in gravy, saw the mess drooping from the edges of our forks and just had to laugh.

Shopping for furniture for the house was complicated, too. The Mission had strict guidelines for furniture and housing: basic/modest. Unlike other missions, ours did not permit furnishings to be shipped from North America. Everything had to be acquired in the country of service so as to fit in with the people of that country. And every item must be basic/modest.

There were no department stores with furniture in stock. A sofa perched outside on the sidewalk announced a shop that constructed sofas and chairs. Inside we were shown pictures of designs and fabric samples. In Canada we didn't dream of ordering custom-made furniture, but in Medellín that was the only way to buy furniture. Searching for used items in the papers, I quickly realized that people did not buy and sell used items as we did in Canada. It would mean allowing strangers into their homes and that was not done.

We felt like royalty, though, as we ordered our sand-coloured sofas, oak bedroom suite and a large oval dining table in light oak to accommodate the frequent guests we would have. It all came out to be extremely economical and within budget. Basic/modest.

There was an upright piano in our suite. After two years without a piano, Matthew and Rebecca enjoyed practicing pieces they remembered. Over lunch one day Harold and I wondered aloud if we should spend our money for a new television to replace the one that was stolen in Costa Rica. Or we could buy a piano.

"A piano!" came the answer from the kids. "We'd rather have a piano, please!"

"Well, I've heard pianos are rare. Hard to find," Harold said. But we started searching for one and started asking around for a good teacher.

During our first weeks in the city an unusual amount of rain fell. It caused a major landslide that destroyed one hundred and twenty homes in a section of Medellín across the city from us. Five hundred Colombians died in the landslide.

I felt torn. While we were ordering furniture to supply our own home, hundreds had lost all their possessions and even their homes.

"My cousins live there and have lost everything!" Mariela told us. "What can we do?" Together with our church people, we gathered clothing and food for the family of her cousins. We loaded dishes and a small fridge into our jeep and drove Mariela with the supplies up the hill, getting as close as we could on the damaged roads.

We found the family in what was left of their tiny adobe brick house. Two of the walls were sheared away, exposing them to public view and to the wind and rain. They had set up a makeshift kitchen that looked to be hanging on the hillside over rough planks. Electric wires were strung from a tall, teetering pole on the street directly to a two-burner stovetop.

The wife and two daughters hugged Mariela and, clearly still in shock, quietly expressed their thanks for the food and other supplies. They were not sure how to respond to us. This was the first time they were meeting foreigners.

When the husband appeared from around the corner, we had our first experience of seeing family conflict due to religious beliefs.

"They are staunch Catholics," Mariela had warned us. Now, when the husband appeared, the wife stepped back and took her distance from Mariela and from us.

The husband stood vigilant and stiff. He did not even glance at us. Looking directly at his wife, he ordered, "Don't get friendly with these *Cristianos!*"

At that time ninety-nine percent of Colombians were Catholic. They referred to themselves as *Católicos* and referred to Protestants as *Cristianos*. Over the years I saw many homes with small signs in their front windows that read *Somos Católicos*, a warning to Protestants to stay away.

Mariela felt embarrassed that we received such treatment from her relatives. We, though, just felt thankful to be spared the landslide and thankful to help in a small way.

I share a joke with the leader of the Colombian Mennonite Brethren Conference.

So much was happening in these first weeks that we felt we were dealing with an avalanche of our own, an avalanche of challenges. We had expected a leisurely, slow start in our work but since there was no pastor, there was no one else in charge, and responsibilities fell to us.

"We're just off the plane!" we complained to each other. "We don't want to take charge."

But challenges came thick and fast. A touring film team asked the church if they could show the Jesus film as an outreach event in the barrio. The church elders said yes. What a shock for us! We found ourselves jumping into a major campaign before we even moved into our own house.

Our dear friends, Trever and Joan Godard, with their young sons came from Cali to welcome us to the country. We had been with them the previous year in language study in Costa Rica and we loved them like family. We all squeezed into the rented suite for a few days. What fun we had reminiscing and laughing over each other's tales of *faux pas* and surprises in the new culture.

"The mission board may be slow on some things," we commiserated together, "but they sure were quick about cutting our salary once we got to Colombia!" Mission salaries were determined according to a cost of living index for the various countries and our pay had dropped to $800 US a month from the $1100 US we'd received while in Costa Rica.

Even so, we looked at the silver lining. "Isn't it great having lots of water in this country and having hot water in good supply?"

"Feels like a luxury, I tell you, after all the struggles with those water tanks in Costa Rica!"

The day after the Godards left we moved into our own home.

Then a day later, in between the many errands to run, the clutch in our jeep went kaput. There seemed to be an obstruction in a line so Harold spent much of the day, right up until midnight trying to fix it. Finally, the next day he went out to buy a new part.

"We feel stretched as far as we can go," I confided in a letter to my parents. "With this outreach campaign coming just when we are moving in and adapting, I feel like an avalanche is upon us and we don't know whether to run with it or try to hold it back. It just looks like the Lord himself is moving this church into action. We've done nothing but pray."

I wished I could focus on organizing the house into a home that reflected our taste but that could not be my priority. In spite of our limited Spanish, the church looked to us for leadership. We were ready and willing to take on anything. We began visiting members in their homes, listening to their stories, praying with them for healing.

Harold had the greater challenge—he was expected to come up with a half hour Spanish sermon for Sunday services. Many evenings he spent in the tiny study bent over Bibles, commentaries and a big Spanish dictionary.

I took on organizing the Sunday School classes and equipping teachers. A meeting of Sunday School teachers was planned for the next week following the morning church service. I offered to bring sandwiches so that we could move into the afternoon meeting right at twelve noon without teachers having to go home for lunch.

That Sunday, I brought a stack of ham sandwiches. Sitting in the morning service I heard the lead elder announce that the teachers' meeting would start after the service at 12:30 or maybe 12:45.

I jumped up from my place in the pew. "No, no," I exclaimed, "we'll start at 12 sharp, as soon as the service is over."

I had a lot to learn about Latin culture!

Later, I told Harold all about it.

"After 12:00, everyone hung around talking in the most casual way. No one acted like there was a meeting to get ready for. I was getting antsy! Mariela had agreed to make juice but it got to be one o'clock by the time she said she was almost ready— just had to buy sugar to put into the juice. So, someone walked to the store to buy sugar.

"There were nine of us. The women made exactly nine cups of juice and portioned it out carefully into nine of those plastic cups. But then Guillo showed up. We hadn't drunk from our cups yet so we all poured our drinks back into a pot. A little water was added and then there were ten cups. Can you believe it, it was 1:30 by the time we *started* our meeting!"

"Acclimatized yet?"

"Very funny. I'm actually really happy with how the meeting turned out. The people are so eager to get this little church alive and vibrant again. It's beautiful."

To become vibrant again there were relationships that needed healing. We wanted to communicate the need for love, for acceptance, for unhindered forgiveness as the way to heal relationships and move forward. And being Mennonites, the best way we knew to promote a family feeling of unity was to gather them together in our own home.

We invited the whole church for an open house the very next Sunday in our new home.

7   It's okay, Señora

"You did what?!" asked an ex-pat American woman I was getting to know. "Open house? You're crazy! An invitation to have your stuff stolen, that's what it is. They'll cart off the kids' toys. Your jewelry. What are you thinking?"

She didn't understand.

We were the only foreign people in our church and that was why we wanted to show the church people how we lived so that there would be no secrets and they could begin to feel comfortable with us. We invited all the people that attended the church.

The American woman's viewpoint was common among foreigners but it was also the view of Colombians themselves. Over the more than forty years of violence, trust between Colombians, even next-door neighbours, had eroded.

"We can't remember a time when we've enjoyed peace," Colombians told us.

Civil war had waged on and off in Colombia since 1948. Back then the conflict between Conservatives and Liberals touched off a bloodbath throughout the country. During *La Violencia*, from 1948-1958, more than 200,000 Colombians were murdered, nearly two thousand *each month*.

The butchering of children and old people, the disembowelling of women led to a frenzied lust for vengeance. Violence became a habit.

Ongoing political disagreements spawned four different revolutionary armies, each known by their initials. The ELN (*Ejército Liberación Nacional*), EPL (*Ejército Popular de Liberación*), M-19

(*Movimiento de 19 de Abril*), and the largest one, FARC (*Fuerzas Armadas Revolucionarias de Colombia*).

Some of these groups had formed in the 1950s among university students; others were inspired by Fidel Castro, fired by Communist ideals. They had since evolved to include many rural people who saw guerrilla action as the only voice they would ever have to call the attention of government to the poverty and injustice in their lives.

Colombians had seen their country torn apart by massacres, kidnappings, corruption and mafia strong-arm tactics. It tore the trust out of people's hearts. Neighbours suspected neighbours. Rather than being neighbourly, families kept to themselves in their heavily barred homes, suspicious of every stranger passing by.

Asira, our housekeeper when we first arrived, a single mom with a son, explained to me that her neighbourhood was one of the dangerous ones.

"Listen, taxis won't go up into my barrio after dark. From our own window, my son has watched someone being killed in front of our house."

"Oh Asira, I'm so sorry. That's a terrible thing. You must be worried for him."

"I'm so worried for him. He's suffering from ulcers already and is only twelve years old!"

Our house was on the west side of the city in the barrio Simón Bolívar, between Carrera 81 and Carrera 84. It fit the Mission policy of basic/modest. The houses on our street stood in attached rows as they did throughout Colombian cities. And as on most streets in Medellin, the row of houses climbed a rise with each successive house slightly higher than the previous one. Ours was near the middle of the hill.

Our house in Simon Bolivar, Medellín. Garage on the left, *sala* on the right. Upstairs, the boys' bedroom behind the balcony on the left, Rebecca's room on the right.

Each house was identical with a garage on one side of its front door and a living room window on the other. Bedrooms upstairs. At the back was a concrete patio that held the clotheslines and beside that a bit of grass with a lemon tree. Each house also had a tiny patch of grass in front of the living room window. In ours stood a tall, spindly palm tree, like some stoic sentinel. The driveway that ran alongside this piece of grass was too short to hold the length of our jeep. Its hindquarters hung over onto the sidewalk.

But there was a sidewalk. In the poorer barrios, the houses opened directly onto the street. We had briefly considered living in a poorer barrio but common sense had prevailed. Our crew of fair-haired children would not have stood a chance at survival there.

I remembered my mother telling how, when I was a baby, my parents had accepted the pastorage of a church in the inner city of Winnipeg. In that neighbourhood drunks roamed the streets and slept on the sidewalks. My dad had wanted to move in next door to the church but it was one of the few times my mother put her foot down.

"I could do that," my mother said, "if we didn't have children. Our children must not pay the price for what we choose to do." I'm the third of my seven siblings and I've always been thankful for my parents' decision to raise us in a safer neighbourhood.

In spite of warnings from well-meaning people we went ahead and planned our open house. No one in the church had a vehicle so Harold rented a bus to carry the group to our house. About twenty adults and a dozen children came, all freshly scrubbed and spotless in their Sunday clothes.

The men and teenage boys gathered with Harold and Matthew in the sala while I took the women and children on a full tour of the house, starting upstairs with the bedrooms, the bathrooms, then Harold's tiny study downstairs and the laundry patio called the *pila*. As was the custom, our pila consisted of a built-in concrete sink and concrete washboard under the open sky.

Then they squeezed into my tiny kitchen to see how foreigners cooked. They marveled that we dried the dishes and stored them behind closed cupboard doors. In their own kitchens, dishes were washed with strong soap under cold running water and set on metal holders above the sink where they drip-dried between meals.

I also had an electric coffee maker while they made their daily *café* by pouring boiling water several times through a cloth bag stuffed with coffee grounds. I had tasted their coffee made that way at church meetings. It was delicious! I wondered how they achieved that.

After the tour, the young boys, whose usual toys were sticks and stones, took down every single toy from the shelves in the boys' room and kept busy with cars and trucks.

In Becky's room, the girls lined up her toy ponies and Barbie dolls across the bed and laid out all the accessories, admiring each piece. I smiled to see that. Our friends in North America thought of us as those poor missionaries. To these Colombians, though, we were those rich foreigners.

Rebecca and a friend with Barbies and ponies.

I had platters of sandwiches, coconut cake and peanut butter cookies spread on the dining room table. You couldn't buy peanut butter in any store in Medellín but one of our church women made it in her home to sell to foreigners. I wanted to give her all the business I could.

I was so new and so ignorant of the customs that I invited them all to help themselves to the food. But no one moved toward the table.

"You go first, you go first," the women whispered shyly, nudging my arm.

"But you're my guests, you go first," I answered.

"But we don't know what to do. You show us."

So, feeling foolish, I placed a sandwich, two cookies and a slice of cake on a plate and handed it to one of the older women. Then each woman followed suit, making an identical plate for each of her own family members. I hadn't learned yet that in the homes of the poor everything is portioned out and they know no other method of taking food than to have the women dole it out on each person's plate.

I poured café con leche for grownups and juice for the kids. Harold brought out his guitar, handed it to Guillermo and soon everyone was singing and clapping.

After dark they piled back onto the bus, laughing and talking, full of treats. Andy and Conrad put their toys back on the shelves. Becky and I wandered through the rooms of our house. We found nothing missing. Not a toy nor piece of jewellery.

A surge of warm feeling for our church people flooded through me. Yes, I could now say "our" people. A community. A family feeling was taking shape.

8 School in the coffee plantation

For the two years before arriving in Colombia, our kids had already attended new schools—first in California, then in Costa Rica.

In my own school years, since my dad was a pastor who moved about, I attended six different schools. For me, shy at the time, that was hell. I was happy to see that our kids were game for another new school experience and making new friends. They donned their backpacks and carried their lunch boxes off to their new classrooms. Conrad, only three going on four, and with a December birthday, was sad to have to wait another year before starting school.

I felt great relief to see our kids come home after their first day of class full of praise and excitement for the new school.

"We can build forts in the trees!"

"At recess we played soccer—everyone together—the grade twelves and the little guys in grade one and two. Everyone plays together!"

Run by the Canadian Baptists for missionary children, the small school stood on a hillside outside the city, beyond the barrio called Bello. Originally a missionary compound, it was an expansive acreage with rows of coffee plants and banana trees. The school building and several houses for teachers stood tucked away here and there among stands of tall bamboo.

The approach to this *finca* was a narrow trail that snaked up a hill. Cars could make it, but jeeps were best. The lane ended in a track marked by two rows of bricks laid in the dirt. This bit of track leading to the gate was on a steep incline and we'd gear the jeep down to first and then rev up to reach the gate.

There was often a cow or two, head down, concentrating on clumps of grass sticking up between the bricks on the road. They were veteran Colombian cows, fearless. It took a good deal of loud honking right at their rear ends to even get them to raise their heads in curiosity before they finally shuffled off.

The gate to the *finca* was locked at all times but honking brought the *mayordomo* running to open up. Inside, the property was lush with greenery. Clumps of tall bamboo, dozens of mango and orange trees and beyond them the expanse of the coffee plantation on the hillside.

Among the trees was a structure with the grandiose name of "gymnasium," a bare concrete shell with tin roof that served as a court for floor hockey and basketball.

The school, called *Alta Vista*, was a long, narrow brick building with a covered walkway along the side facing the hill. The doors to the five rooms opened directly onto this walkway. There were four classrooms and a tiny staff room. All twelve grades were taught in the four classrooms. The entire high school shared one room while grades one to six doubled up in the other three rooms.

Rebecca, right, at her desk at the Alta Vista School.

There was no computer and no science lab. There were battered brown desks, plenty of maps and posters, and blackboards. One of the classrooms doubled as library with stacks lining the wall. These were packed with English books, many of them salvaged from school libraries in Canada. They'd been shipped down by well-meaning folk and arrived by the musty boxful, each book stamped DISCARDED. But who cared that they were old? They were a goldmine of English words in a foreign land.

High school teacher, Trevor McMonagle, in the classroom that doubled as library.

During recess and noon hour students were free to roam the open fields or to organize a game of baseball or touch football. Our kids loved to climb the mango trees, build forts of bamboo stalks, and play hide and seek. The bus ride to school was long and cramped, along streets clouded with diesel fumes, but the prospect of the blissful freedom of playing outdoors kept our children content.

Two years before our arrival in Medellín, a guerrilla group had stolen down the hillside and invaded the school. No one had been hurt. This had seemingly not traumatized the kids or teachers. After a few days of cancelled classes, school had resumed as though the invasion had been a mere inconvenience. We hoped that experience would never be repeated.

But there were other surprises. When we were new to Medellín, during the very first week of school, a notice was sent home. "School is cancelled for tomorrow. Because of the assassinations, protests and general unrest, it is too dangerous for North Americans to cross the city to Bello."

School resumed the following day, though, as if a snowstorm had caused the closure and not a blizzard of violence.

All the teachers and the principal, Bob Rempel, were Canadian. I never heard a bad word from our kids about any of their teachers, only praise. Becky and Andy both had young single women who had bravely come from Canada to teach in Colombia. Matthew's English teacher, Trevor McMonagle, spoke French and Matthew was thrilled to hear he could study both Spanish and French. Matthew enjoyed setting goals for himself and Mr. McMonagle inspired him by setting ever-higher standards, turning out to be the perfect teacher for him. With his help, Matthew was soon memorizing a string of Bible verses in French.

Instruction started for our children before they left home in the morning. At the breakfast table, while the kids had their bun and hot chocolate, Harold read the devotional for the day. He liked to insert little trick comments and false wordings into the Bible readings to keep the kids engaged and interested.

"Cast your bread upon the waters," he read, "and— it will sink to the bottom."

"No!" the kids would call out. "It will come again!"

If he read, "Be sure to lay up treasures for yourselves on earth—" the kids would correct him by saying, "In heaven. In heaven, not earth. Silly."

Sometimes I cautioned, "We don't want the kids to think the Bible is a book to make fun of." But he continued, keeping it fun for himself, not just for the kids. And, maybe, to help counteract his wife's seriousness.

While the older kids eagerly went off to school, I was relieved that Conrad adjusted well to playing at home alone. Between constructing with Lego or playing with the dog Mitzi, we often did a bit of schoolwork, pages of numbers and colours.

One day, reflecting on that day's Bible reading, he asked me how Jesus could shrink enough to get into his heart. I explained how we can't see the wind but we see the leaves move on the lemon tree in the backyard and that is the wind. After that, whenever the leaves moved he pointed outside and said, "There's God again!"

I also explained that God speaks to us and if we listen carefully we can learn what to do. So, the next morning he did a number of helpful little tasks for me. After each job he said, "Jesus told me to do that."

But when he got tired of helping, he announced, "Now Jesus said he wants to get out of my heart." And away he went on his merry way.

We bought a tricycle for Conrad to ride on the sidewalk, thinking he could enjoy the outdoors and meet neighbourhood children. But we saw no other children outdoors. So, when Conrad was out on the tricycle I always kept watch from the tiny balcony.

"Stay just here in front of these two houses. No going any further."

But even then, the woman next door stepped out and called up to me, "What do you mean letting your child play outside? Do you want his bike stolen? Do you want him kidnapped? Only *mal-educados* play outdoors."

Sigh.

"Sorry Conrad, but soon you'll go to school with the other kids and then you'll have lots of fun there climbing trees. Hey, let's practice— let's go see how high you can climb on the lemon tree in our patio."

 ## 9   Is that a gun at the window?

In early October the campaign was launched to show the Jesus film *The Life of Christ* out of doors. We were fully involved and yet felt in a state of mild shock. We barely knew the church people yet, nor their customs, never mind understanding their neighbours who were largely unsympathetic to their beliefs.

A few blocks from the church we hung a sheet from someone's balcony and the projector was set up on the balcony of a house across the street. When the film began to roll, people from the community gathered on the street below.

When the film ended, the people were invited to leave their names and addresses if they had questions and wanted a visit at their home.

"Sixty requests for home visits!" We were staggered.

When would we ever visit that many people?

We already knew that finding addresses in Medellín was difficult. Besides that, many homes didn't have phones and so calling ahead was impossible. I moaned about this in a letter home.

"One afternoon a church woman and I set out for the first time to find some of the homes on the inquiry cards. We walked for half an hour before finding the first address and the person wasn't home! After three hours of climbing up and down steep streets, we found only one woman at home! How many months will it take to find sixty people?"

To find these people I began to regularly take the bus to the Salvador barrio. I met up with Elsa, one of our church women who also took two buses to get to church. Together we walked up and down the narrow dusty streets in search of addresses on the response cards. Sometimes we visited our female parishioners who were sick or troubled.

A street in the Salvador barrio.

I looked to Elsa as my mentor. A respected leader in the church, she was ten years older than me and lived with her husband and sons in a two-bedroom concrete box in row housing. Her life was a daily challenge. There were times when she sang or prayed in church that I saw tears roll down her face.

Elsa and I walked down streets where often women would be seated in open doorways, visiting with neighbours or watching young children play on the street. In this barrio, children played outdoors. Inside the narrow houses, ceilings were high and the air was cooler than outside. If there was a *sala*, it usually held a Spanish-style aging couch, the wood scratched and the inevitable red velvet cushions worn and faded to pink.

Where poverty prohibited even that, in the rented rooms of the very poor we would be invited to sit on a single bed loosely covered with a sheet while the hostess found a low stool to sit on. Faded prints of the Sacred Heart or the Blessed Virgin and Child covered some of the cracks in the walls. For those who had converted to Protestantism, a favorite print was of Christ knocking on a massive wooden door, the door of Everyman's heart.

One afternoon Elsa and I met at the church where we locked up our purses. Then I followed her out to the street, both of us in light cotton dresses ready for hours under the hot sun. Smoking buses careened past us down the steep streets raising clouds of dust. We picked our way past old men gambling, squatted over a Parcheesi board on the sidewalk in the shade. They looked up at our hips and muttered comments I felt blessed to not understand.

Somewhere nearby I heard firecrackers booming and buses backfiring. A typical Medellín afternoon.

Soon we found ourselves on a short street, one block long that ended abruptly at a cliff. An uneven stairway of concrete steps, black with age, led up this rock, connecting the street to a maze of adobe brick houses at the top. Elsa figured the address we wanted ran along the top of that hill.

As soon as we turned the corner into the street, we sensed something was wrong.

Lining the bluff at the end of the street atop the stairs stood a crowd of people. They were oddly silent, staring down on the street and on us as though waiting for something. But there was nothing to see. The street was narrow, with no sidewalks, the doors of the houses opening right onto the street.

And we two women were the only people on the street.

"Something is strange here," whispered Elsa, slowing her pace.

Then I noticed that every door and window shutter was closed up tight. In spite of the heat. No dogs lay on doorsteps. No women stood in the doorways. Only a heavy, eerie silence.

I felt Elsa tense up.

As we walked forward my eyes swept the row housing.

I gasped.

One window shutter stood ajar, the barrel of a rifle poking out. My heart started to pound. I didn't know if Elsa had seen it too, but I wasn't about to point to it.

"Pray, *hermana!*" she whispered without turning her head. She must have seen.

I felt a great impulse to run, to race to the stairs up ahead and leap up them as fast as possible. But along with the impulse came a vision of myself stupidly crashing on the stairs, maybe with a bullet in my back.

We slowly put one foot in front of the other. The watching crowd stood silent like a circus audience held captive by a tightrope walker.

We passed the house with the gunman at the window. Did he really swing the barrel to keep us in his sights? I didn't dare swivel my eyes to see.

Finally, we neared the steps, and then painfully climbed them. When we reached the top, an old, toothless woman stepped forward and threw open her arms to us, beaming.

"Thank God you're alive!"

Then others called out to us and some patted our shoulders.

"What's going on here?" Elsa asked.

"We've been having a big shootout! *Un tiroteo*. Bang, bang from one side of the street to the other."

So, the noises we'd heard earlier were not just firecrackers.

"*Sí, sí!* A shootout," other voices joined in. "And do you know when they stopped? Just when you came around the corner. *Ave Maria!* We're here waiting now to see how many dead there are. But you're not dead. *Dios mio!* God protected you!"

Tiroteo. Shootout. That was a common household word I had already learned after just weeks in the country. Gangs settling their differences with guns.

I breathed a big sigh of relief. Elsa and I gave each other a reassuring hug. Then we moved away from the crowd and continued up the street along the top of the bluff.

Elsa stopped and looked at me. "Would you like to go home now?" she asked. "We can do the visiting another day."

"No. No, let's just keep going. It would be a waste to quit now."

We kept hunting for obscure addresses. Of the five houses we aimed for that day, we found only two where the people were home. Not a bad result for an afternoon in the barrio, especially since we felt we had been able to answer urgent questions of those we visited.

Later that afternoon, about six o'clock, we collected our purses from the church and boarded a crowded bus. Elsa confided to me, "Do you know what? Visiting that woman who had nothing in her house except a single bed, that made me thankful for my home. I'm happy to go home now and make supper in my little kitchen."

I was very thankful, too, to reach my own home that evening. How safe and happy it was! What a spoiled foreigner I was—I could leave this troubled land if I wanted to and fly to a safe haven. But the Colombian women lived with the pain of danger from the cradle to the grave. I felt great admiration for them persevering day after day, working to keep their kids out of gangs, working toward a better future.

"Harold, ask me if I'm acclimatized yet."

"Are you?"

"No way. Surprises around every corner."

 ## 10   Let me on this bus

"I cannot change that bill," insisted the bus driver.

"Why not?" asked the passenger, pointing to a full tray of coins on the dashboard. "You have the change right there."

The fare was the equivalent of ten cents. For some reason the driver had chosen to be insulted by the offer of a "big" bill of two hundred pesos, worth about eighty cents. He had refused the bill and now he couldn't back down without losing face.

While they argued, I hung out the doorway, my hair flying in the wind, the asphalt speeding by below me. I couldn't get past the turnstile because the passenger ahead of me—a man dressed in linen pants and white shirt, buttons open down the front, macho style—refused to budge.

He stood planted, his hand extended with the bill. He repeated flatly, "You have the change right there. Why don't you change it?"

"I will *not* change it," insisted the driver, a burly man with a potbelly. "You should be more considerate. I have to save my change for an emergency."

My arms aching from holding on, I wanted to shout, "Soon I may supply you with that emergency!"

The passenger stood statue-still repeating his phrase and showing no signs of weakening. A classic standoff. I had heard of bus drivers pulling out their gun at cars that cut them off or at passengers who offended them. I was getting nervous.

The driver raised his voice. "You're so inconsiderate! Look at this poor *señora*." He pointed his nose in my direction. "She can't get into the bus simply because you won't give me the correct change."

The passenger did not even glance in my direction. He kept his eye fixed on the driver and insisted he get change. If only I could let go one hand to dig in my purse, I decided, I would happily pay the man's fare myself!

Fortunately, the showdown ended. Eventually, the driver gave in, probably realizing he couldn't pick up more passengers with the doorway blocked. I was able to enter the sanctuary of the bus at last.

I often took a bus across the city to visit the church women though I didn't expect to actually get to sit down in buses. They usually came heavily packed. Often men were hanging out of the doorway. When the driver saw me signal at the roadside, he would slow to a crawl. The men would jump down, and run alongside, still clutching the hand bar. I would rush to mount the bottom step and get swooped up to join the mass in the bus's belly. It tested my coordination.

The Colombian buses were rich in colour. Bright red seats. The windows and ceiling dripped with rows of red fringe that swayed back and forth as the bus lumbered forward. Over the front window hung a statue of the Blessed Virgin and a wooden crucifix heavy with thorns and agony. The money box, not a box but rather a red plastic silverware tray, rested on the large motor casing. The various denominations of coins and bills sat neatly separated in the sections designed for forks and spoons.

In a crowded bus normal modesty was brushed aside. Even when there was standing room only, the bus kept stopping and new passengers keep boarding. The aisle crowds got more and more tightly packed. I sometimes had my thigh pressed into the shoulder of a man in an aisle seat for thirty minutes with no possibility of adjusting my stance.

But if by chance the person seated next to where I stood would get up to leave the bus, then I became the lucky owner of a seat. But, of course, even though my feet were aching I must not be seated immediately after the other passenger vacated. I must acknowledge the local custom, allow thirty seconds or so to pass so that the seat could cool and so that the germs and evil spirits dissipated. Then I could sit. One *never* sits on a warm seat.

The day of the standoff between driver and passenger was a day that I wanted to get out of the house because it was the day the maid came. I planned pastoral visits when she was there because I couldn't bear to stay in the house with her.

For fourteen years I'd been a housewife in Canada and perfectly capable of doing all the cleaning, laundry and cooking while caring for the children. In Colombia, though, everyone who could afford it had some sort of house help. A maid was a necessity because every window in the house had a section of louvres set in concrete, permanently open. Dust and dirt blew in freely over all surfaces. The tile floors were swept and wet-mopped every other day. Clothes, all cotton, were hung to dry and all needed ironing. Also, with no instant, canned or frozen foods and no mixes, I spent long hours preparing meals.

In this society of classes, I was viewed as perching at the top of the heap solely because I was a foreigner from a wealthy country. It made no difference that in my own country I was middle class from a poor minister's home. No matter that I had put myself through college scrubbing floors on my knees for a fussy woman who stood over me and dictated that the rag be circled counter-clockwise each time, never the other way around.

So of course, I had a maid. I was happy to give her employment but I could only bear to have her come two days a week. Wherever I wanted to be, that's where she inevitably showed up. If I sat down on the sofa, she swept under my feet. If I mixed a casserole in the kitchen, she looked over my shoulder.

"That much salt you put in! You'll be thirsty for a week!"

If I escaped to the bedroom for a delicious hour with a mystery book, the maid would show up to wash the floor and chat, chat, chat. I hadn't learned how to be a fearsome señora, to give silent icy glares or to order her out of the room. I usually took the coward's solution and escaped from the house for several hours.

This day there was even more reason to escape since in a weak moment I'd consented to the maid's six-year-old nephew, Arsenio, coming to play at our house during a day off from his school.

To go out, I was dressed in red slacks, khaki shirt and a red leather belt. I thought my red sandals were the perfect way to complete the outfit. As I said goodbye to the maid and walked to the front door, little Arsenio called out, *"Señora, los zapatos!"* Your shoes!

"Hush boy," Asira said, "that's how the foreign lady goes out on the street." He kept staring, sure I had forgotten to change my footwear. Colombian women wore only proper shoes to go out, usually high heels, never sandals or flip-flops. Only tourists wore sandals. It took me a year to learn that.

Arsenio chattered even more than his aunt.

"Why do you wear slacks instead of a skirt?" he asked me. His crowning question came when he heard me fish for the correct Spanish word in conversation with Asira.

"Why do you speak funny?" he asked.

"I'm still learning new Spanish words," I said.

"I'm only six and I can speak no problem."

I laughed.

"Good logic! Give that boy another cookie." Away he went for the cookie and I slipped out into the sunshine. Freedom. And even the struggle to board the bus could not steal my joy.

11   Meet Napoleon next door

Unlike our experience in the prairie town we came from, we met no neighbours over the back fence. Back fences were concrete blocks stacked eight to ten feet high. And as neighbours, we were as suspect as strangers.

"If you want to be a good neighbour," we were told, "just mind your own business."

Soon after we moved into our house I stepped across the small patch of grass to ring the neighbour's doorbell. Their house, joined to ours with a common wall, looked identical to ours.

A maid in a yellow uniform with a clean white apron unlocked the door and invited me in. The lady of the house soon hurried in to welcome me. Her name was Constanza, about fifteen years older than me, with soft features, erect carriage, a feminine dress, nylons and high heels.

Oh, what a *schlep* I was! I wore sandals and cotton slacks, the clothes I thought suitable for a tropical climate. But in true Colombian style, her graciousness never faltered.

"*Como estás!* What an honour to have you visit."

She led me into the sala where a thick carpet in a red paisley design dominated the room bordered by couches. The wooden arms, legs and back of the couch were covered in fancy scrollwork. Three thick cushions in red velvet formed the seat and three more the back. These Spanish-style couches were ubiquitous. I had seen very old versions of these in the homes of poor folk we'd visited.

Constanza took a seat across from me, folded one beautiful slim leg behind the other and leaned forward with eager eyes, "Do you like it in Medellín?" she asked. "Why did you move here? Where do the children go to school?"

I leaned forward too, eager to converse and pleased to find Spanish words rolling off my tongue without much effort. Two lovely teenage daughters joined us. They shook my hand and sat beside each other on another couch. Like so many Colombian young women, they were beautiful with gentle, gracious manners.

Then entered the husband.

Enrique was a full head shorter than his wife. He took a seat in a side chair, his feet not reaching the floor. He greeted me in a voice that I found as shrill and high-pitched as a dentist's drill.

Though I didn't know then that he beat his wife, I detected an aggressive manner and felt immediately on guard.

Constanza excused herself to see about the coffee and Enrique launched into a lecture.

"We have very high standards in education here. In my youth I had to study Greek and Latin in order to get through university. Did you know that Bogotá, the capital city, is called the Athens of Latin America?"

"No. How wonderful."

He went on. "Colombia has more than forty universities. Of course, most are in Bogotá. Have you been to Bogotá?"

I shook my head. "We just moved here a short while ago so we haven't seen anything but Medellín so far."

"Not even Cartagena? You must go to Cartagena! There's a lot of history there. Our culture derives from the courts of Spain in the 1700s. We have a lot of respect for history."

I understood his point. Unlike Canada, this was not a society of immigrants, of farmers or refugees who had pulled themselves up by their bootstraps. Colombians valued graciousness and beauty.

Constanza entered just then with a soft step and regal bearing. Behind her came the maid with an enormous silver tray covered in embroidered lace. On it stood a silver coffee pot, silver sugar bowl and five delicate gray-blue demitasse cups each on its tiny saucer. Heavy silver coffee spoons lay on large hand-embroidered linen napkins.

Like other Colombians I later met, Constanza delighted in making the coffee time an elegant affair. I felt transported to the parlour of some count in a Dostoevsky novel.

Darn my cotton slacks! And I couldn't help but compare this occasion with coffee times in Canada. There, it was so casual. "Care for coffee?" "Sure"— and coffee was sloshed into the nearest convenient mug.

But here Constanza asked with great deference, "May I pour you some *tinto*?"

"What trouble you've gone to just for me," I responded. "This looks wonderful! *Gracias*. You're very kind."

Rich black coffee was poured. I added three spoons of sugar, following the custom. Along with the coffee came thick slices of *ponque*, a dense, not-too-sweet cake. No frosting. This is a Colombian standby, a version of pound cake, and I fell in love with it. It was the perfect accompaniment to heavy, sweet coffee.

Coffee cup in hand, Enrique continued to hold forth. Full steam ahead. I was sad to see that no female in the house dared break in. The wife and daughters sat erect on the couches gazing at me wistfully. I especially wished I could talk with the daughters, as young people were my favourite people to talk with.

"Now, please do not think that Medellín was always the way you find it now," Enrique declared. "*De ninguna manera!* No way! Not many years ago we could leave our doors unlocked all day. We could leave a lawn chair in the front yard, go inside for dinner and come out to find it still there."

He added, "As you say in English, *No problem.* But now we can't even leave a heavy plant on the second-floor balcony. You lie down, close your eyes for a siesta and the plant is taken! Disappeared! Four of us here on our street have had our plants stolen from balconies in the last month. I mean tall palms in heavy planters. How do they do it? Very bad. Very bad."

Constanza sat with her hands tightly folded. She ventured, "And what do you miss about the United States?"

Enrique exploded. "She's not *gringa*!" He shouted. "She's not *gringa*! She's from Canada!" Constanza shrank back in silence.

He lit a cigarette and leaned forward, his tone softening. "Listen, *señora*, why did you come here? What does your husband do?"

"My husband's a teacher. Of geography and also music, in voice and choir. During the summers he taught water sports at camps: canoeing, sailing and wind-surfing."

"He will teach those things here, then?"

"No, no. This is different. This is a career change for us. We are both Bible teachers now and we work in a church here."

"Which church?"

"A church in the barrio of Salvador near downtown."

"*Sí, Sí, yo sé.* I know that barrio. But why work there? Those people are not worth it! They are thieves. They won't work, expecting handouts and more handouts. Lazy people!"

"The people we work with hold jobs. They work hard to earn enough to live on."

"In drugs and prostitution, eh? Ha, ha!"

"The people we work with can't even afford bicycles," I explained. "It would be hard to believe they're involved in drug sales."

We did work with some prostitutes, but that was not information for him. We were on a topic now in which we wouldn't see eye to eye. I was wary of offending my host, committing a cultural blunder.

"You are educated people," he bleated. "You are wasting your time there!"

"And you, what do you do?" I asked.

He leaned back in his chair, his short legs rising higher off the floor. "I am a military doctor. Retired now." He sucked hard on his cigarette. "I've worked in many places in Colombia. On the mountains, in the savannah, in the jungle. Right here in Medellín is the best place. Perfect climate."

"Yes," I smiled, relieved to be agreeing with him. "Your climate is ideal. One doesn't even need a sweater at night. Coming from Canada, you can imagine how much we appreciate your wonderful weather."

I was happy to be able to part on agreeable terms with this man who was so brusque, so different from other Colombians I met.

"Harold! I met the neighbours! He's a regular little Napoleon but he's got the nicest wife. I think we'll be friends."

His wife did continue as a gracious neighbour. I wish I could have done more to lessen her suffering. She is, to me, a picture of Colombia's grace and kindness.

12   What am I doing here?

Over the years I made many personal visits to women, young and old, each visit bringing some new surprise. But I'll never forget how confused and baffled I felt in my first visit to Lily. She was a pretty girl, about eighteen, a baptized member of our church. She had been excommunicated, though, for getting pregnant out of marriage. That was harsh treatment. Yet in 1988, that is what seemed right to the church elders.

She asked to rejoin the church and the elders decreed that as preparation for re-acceptance she would have to meet with me, the missionary, each week for Bible study and counselling. That was the wisdom of the church at the time.

I did not look forward to this task and was putting it off. But then Lily called me one day, speaking in a whisper.

"*Señora* Doroti, can you please come visit? My father asked my uncle to kill my boyfriend! He's going to give my uncle money to do it. I'm so scared. Can you please come visit me?"

Though I didn't see how my visit would help, I decided I had to do whatever I could. I flagged a taxi that found its way past horse-drawn carts and belching buses, up the hill to La Milagrosa. I looked at my watch and saw I was at Lily's house right at the time we'd agreed on. It was a poor barrio with no space between the street and the house door. Two boys jumped up from where they had been sitting on the dusty paved shoulder of the road.

"Welcome *señora*. We are Lily's brothers. She'll be here soon. *No demora!*" They ushered me into the *sala* that held the usual red couch and two straight-backed chairs. I contented myself with chatting with the boys.

The older one, just finishing high school, was slated to enter compulsory military service. Oh, I felt sad that such young guys had to become soldiers. But Colombia, they said, needed the military strength. This was two months after we had arrived in Medellín and terrorism and mafia activity had hit a new high.

"How do you feel about this declaration of civil war that the government announced this week?" I asked.

He shook his head. "I'm very, very sad. I don't want to be in the army. I wanted to go for more studies."

"And you wanted to enjoy the weekends," teased his brother. "Enjoy the weekends with—"

"I'm not ready to go out to fight in a civil war. And maybe even be called to make the ultimate sacrifice." *El último sacrificio.*

Now Lily entered the room with Bible and study book in hand. The brothers went back outside and she sat beside me on the couch. She began to tell me in a low voice her struggles over the past week. Her fear for her boyfriend's life. Her fear for her own safety. Her confusion.

About ten minutes into our conversation a motorcyclist pulled up outside the open door to deliver a huge bag full of stuffed animals. Lily and her mother sold these from home. Lily got up, took the bag and opened it to examine the merchandise. Other family members of various ages appeared and each stuffed toy was handled and admired by everyone, including me. Just as the toys were being put away again, Lily's mother arrived home.

"Oh, let's see if everything is right. I'm the one with the price list. I'll get it and we'll check." Then, each animal was handled again with care and examined as to its worth and expense.

Chapter 12

By this time, an hour had passed and I had hardly begun any meaningful conversation. Lily suggested we go to another room.

"No, no," her mother said, "we, the family, will go to the back of the house." They all went off except for two small pre-school girls who chose to stay and bother us. For the next hour they pinched and hit each other, grabbed Lily's pen, and delighted in imitating the words she spoke. Serious conversation was difficult.

I was feeling upset with the naughtiness of the girls and had to talk to myself. *Dorothy, you're new to the culture. You've still got to observe, not interfere. And you know the Colombian way is to give kids freedom to develop self-assertiveness and self-determination. It's their only chance for that. From adolescence on, Colombian society calls for conformity and acquiescing to elders.*

I bit my tongue.

Then, a third brother arrived home. I made the traditional greetings and small talk with him. He was followed closely by two cousins on a motorcycle. They drove the motorcycle right through the door into the house, through the *sala* and on into the next room where they began to repair something on it.

In spite of interruptions, we kept up our conversation. Lily surprised me when her eyes filled with tears. "I do want to live a better life. I want to be stronger in myself."

In walked another cousin, off the street, and Lily, still in tears, introduced me. A fellow emerged from the other room carrying the motorcycle fender. Together these two mounted a bicycle leaning by the doorway.

"We're off! We're going to find the best deal possible to fix that crazy bike!"

Lily and I continued our chat about spiritual matters. Then one of the little girls dropped an empty glass. It shattered on the concrete floor. Lily shouted, the girls cried. I picked up the splinters while Lily settled the two little girls down.

Soon after that, Lily's older sister with her husband arrived at the door carrying what looked to be a motor of some kind. We greeted them and the sister passed through to the kitchen. Her husband sat down on the floor next to a power outlet and began to work on the motor by sticking stripped wires directly into the electrical outlet to test it.

What a circus. I've been here two hours and what's been accomplished? I know that in the barrios there is little chance of privacy, but this is mayhem.

I should have been upset. Instead, I don't know why, but I felt compassion. My diary reads, "I left Lily's house with a deepened desire to remain always in Colombia to minister to these barrio folks, so bound by old habits and many fears."

Later, I learned that the parade of relatives had been intentional. By meeting me, each one became a witness to the fact that a foreign missionary was looking out for Lily. And they used that fact to prevent the father and uncle from carrying out their plans for murder.

 ## 13   The police don't come

Police were occupied with serious matters so Colombians didn't bother to report theft. Robbery was rampant in Medellín. It never crossed our minds to report it either. But a few incidents made it into my diary.

"In the past weeks a neighbour's car on our street was stolen outside their house. Our next-door neighbour's daughter's car was stolen too. Both at gunpoint. A neighbour's balcony things were robbed and another house on our street was broken into.

"A few blocks from us on the street where the Wiests live, their two neighbours were forced to surrender cars at gunpoint. And someone climbed up Wiest's balcony and stole their tape recorder in the afternoon in full view of neighbours who took no action. Such things are sure to be happening throughout this city where law and order are slipping away."

Mail for us arrived at a box in a downtown post office. Harold stopped there frequently on his way to and from other appointments. Though he was away from the vehicle only a few minutes to get the mail, on several occasions our jeep was broken into and items stolen.

One day, on his way to play soccer with the church youth, he stopped for the mail and his equipment bag was stolen from the vehicle. He came home very sad.

"I can't believe how quick those thieves are! They're just hanging around waiting for vehicles to park there. Now we have to buy new stuff for the youth group."

Another day it was my turn to feel sad. I spent a few hours making a delicious beef stew for Carlos's family. He was in hospital with cancer. His wife Angelina would visit him, leaving the kids home alone. I packed the stew, bread and a bag of apples into the back of the jeep and kissed Harold goodbye. The family's house was a poor one sitting high up on a shantytown hillside, far from the hospital. So, on the way to deliver the stew, Harold stopped at the hospital to pick up Angelina. The jeep was locked when he ran in to get her, but that did not stop the thieves. They took the stereo and tape player as well as construction tools. But what made me saddest was my lovely stew and bag of apples—gone!

"It makes me feel sick," I wrote a friend, "but we just learn to accept it apathetically. It saps the energy from us, though."

Another effect it had—it made Colombians suspicious of everyone, especially strangers. I recorded one of our experiences in my diary.

"Last night Harold brought home a stranger, a guy who showed up for the first time at church asking for help. His name is Marco. I was not very happy about Harold bringing him into our house. Who knew what he was up to?

"Marco, who looks about 20, says he's from Ecuador. Says he traveled to Colombia from Ecuador and had all his stuff stolen here, including documents. So, he was in a real bind. Looks naïve and in shock. Because of the violence, people in Medellín are so suspicious that even the church people wouldn't believe him or help him. In fact, ours was the third or fourth church he'd gone to for help and was always turned away.

"We made a bed for him on the living room floor. Fed him and then I locked all the children's bedroom doors and ours, too. At 5:30 this morning he was still downstairs and no incident. Thank the Lord! Harold drove him to the bus, got him food, paid his fare to Ecuador and saw him get on the bus. Harold says he was very grateful."

Theft was one thing, but there were also not enough policemen to deal with the many murders. One day a phone call at our house asked for the maid we had then, Maria.

When she hung up she came to me shaking and pale.

"Something terrible happened. They said my son was attacked. I have to go now."

"Your grown son?"

"Yes, twenty-three. *Dios mio!* What's happened?"

Harold was away with the jeep so I gave her taxi money.

We heard nothing for two anxious days. She had no telephone so we couldn't call her nor did we know where she lived. That seems strange to say but it was normal there. People who lived in poor barrios could rarely even tell us their own address. After two days she called.

"*Señora* Doroti, my son was killed."

My heart sank and my words of sympathy felt empty. I felt completely inadequate. As Colombian law required, they had buried him the day after he died, so now the funeral was passed.

I asked if we could come to visit her and she answered an eager, "*Sí, claro que sí!*" I carefully wrote down her address and a maze of descriptions of roads and directions, hoping Harold would be able to decipher the route there.

The next day I prepared some foods for her and Harold and I set off. The jeep jostled and squeaked its way through the city to a poor barrio on the far side. Harold's sixth sense found the way as we nosed into narrow streets, squeezing by cars and trucks to finally pull up on a gravelly street.

Maria's home was built of adobe blocks and looked only partially completed. But it was certainly better than the underground apartments and crowded rooms of some of the people we knew. Geraniums in coffee tins sat on the windowsill and inside a bright cloth covered a small round table.

The room smelled of fresh coffee. We sat on rough wooden chairs and Maria brought us each a demitasse of *tinto*. She had none herself but sat red-eyed on a straight-backed chair. As she told us the story of the past few days, she often broke into sobs.

When her son had been killed, a relative had told her where the body lay.

"I went straight there from your house," she said. "I found him lying on the sidewalk where he fell. *Dios mio!* I waited for the police to come. They had said I couldn't move him until they came. I cried and cried. Every time I heard a car I looked to see if it was the police, but no. They didn't come!" She wiped her tears.

"Oh, I waited," she cried. "I was on my knees over my dear son. Just twenty-three. Only twenty-three. A gang shot him, I know. But the police didn't come. The police didn't come and I couldn't move him myself. They didn't come for four hours. Four hours in that sun!"

She sighed and slumped in her chair. Staring at the floor she continued in a low monotone, "Why should the police come? We have no *importancia*. Someone shoots. Someone dies. The police don't come."

We nodded, speechless. It was terrible beyond words.

I felt helpless and foolish. We offered up prayers. She pressed our hands in gratitude but I felt the gulf between us. If I chose I could fly away to a better place at any time but she had to stay and live out her life in this troubled society.

14   It's teamwork

Praying in Spanish, conversing in Spanish, working continually in Spanish challenged us daily to learn new words and new ways to express ideas. To beef up our language abilities, Harold and I both followed a scheduled program to read through the Bible in Spanish. The plan was to read all the way from Genesis to Revelation in eighteen months. It took much more time than reading in English because we often stopped to search out words in the Spanish dictionary.

We were eagerly waiting for team members to arrive, a missionary couple we came to know while at seminary in California. Finally, in January 1988, five months after we started work in Medellín, the Wiests came to join us with their three beautiful pre-schoolers, Anna, James and Candace.

Their assignment was focused on a different area of the city from where we were working, yet it was wonderful to have friends with whom to discuss work challenges and adjustments to the culture. We were thrilled to see them!

Their first job was to find a suitable house. That would take time. So, they lived with us while the search was on, moving into Rebecca's room, which we used as a guest room. Rebecca camped out on a foamie on the floor in our bedroom.

Conrad now had good playmates during the long hours when our older kids were away at school.

We lived together for four or five weeks. In spite of the cramped quarters we got on very well. They were open, transparent, generous-hearted, and both had a great sense of humour. I only learned later how rare it is for mission teams to get along so well. The Colombians, too, found them very *simpatico*.

A few months later, Albert and Anna Enns, veteran missionaries, moved into an apartment in Medellín to complete the team. The Home Office in North America was beginning a new phase. For the first time they were bringing together workers from different countries to form intercultural teams. The Wiests were Americans, we were Canadians and the Ennses, fluent in Spanish, came from Paraguay.

We felt fortunate to have such a strong team. The Ennses had launched many new churches and had great wisdom and insight into the Latino mindset and yet they were two of the humblest people I've ever met. Years later I was privileged to write their biography in a book I titled *Whatever it Takes*, showing their remarkable lives of escape from violence and the wild and tangled story of how they agreed to marry.

While our assignment was with the church in the barrio of Salvador, the Wiests and the Ennses launched into ministry reaching into other parts of the city. Yet both couples attended our church on Sundays and lent help where needed. As a team we met every Tuesday morning, from eight o'clock to noon, to hear each other's challenges, laugh together and map out strategies.

"You're a godsend," Harold and I told the others. "Without you, how could we do all this stuff?" There were outreach Bible studies, weekly church fellowship groups, pastoring, counselling, training church leaders, figuring out how to teach new converts effectively, training music leaders and visiting new contacts. Whew! And squeezing in family time somewhere as well.

Our mission team: Conrad, Anna Wiest, Rebecca, me, Linda Wiest, Anna Enns, Andy, Albert Enns, Candace, Galen Wiest, Matthew, James Wiest.

The team interactions infused us with new energy. Harold began to think of taking on the construction of a new church sanctuary.

The church people, too, were showing signs of new life. We started weekly home study groups in members' homes. The numbers were steadily going up at Sunday services, at the Saturday youth group and at the weekly women's group. The time came to form a committee to plan the women's meetings.

"You must be president of our women's group," I heard a strong voice announce at a planning meeting. The voice was directed at me. "You have the new ideas so you should be our leader."

"No," I said, "that's how you get into trouble. Missionaries leave— you have to do it yourself."

"But you do it and we'll watch you. We'll learn from you."

"No," I said, "you don't learn by watching, only by doing."

So, Mariela was voted in. Tall, slim Mariela who, when I first met her, was quiet and withdrawn. But she soon came out of her shell and took on a number of church responsibilities. A committee was voted in to support Mariela and things started to really take off. The women came alive with fresh ideas, better than mine, and with the energy to carry them out.

"This is wonderful," I told them. "I love your plan to meet in each other's homes. Much more inviting."

"Now our relatives and neighbours want to come to our meetings. We have a short Bible lesson and then a craft lesson or maybe a cooking class. Of course, in our houses we don't have everything we need for the *café* but we carry over the cups from church."

Those ever-present plastic cups! At church meetings people's faces lit up whenever a tray of those coloured cups appeared. Since coffee with milk would entail the expense of buying milk, it was usually sweet black *tinto* that was served at meetings and events.

Youth group at church

The youth of the church became energized as well. Harold spent time playing soccer with them. And he regularly took his guitar to church to practise music together with the youth on Saturday or Sunday night.

Two youths started a kids' club for children in the neighbourhood around the church. One afternoon on my way to a women's meeting at church, I dropped in unannounced at Freddy's house to see how the kids' club was functioning. I'm glad I didn't know then what was to happen not long after, the horrors that would shatter that family.

But now the old-style house stood calmly shoulder-to-shoulder with its neighbours, all just two steps off the roadway. About fifteen family members lived in this house, though Freddy was the only one attending our church.

It was Freddy who answered my knock. "Oh, sister Doroti, come in please, come in."

The wide wooden door led to the airy patio in the centre of the home. He invited me to sit on one of the two sofas in the patio. As we chatted I could see his mother at work in the kitchen, though she did not greet me. She had not attended any meeting at our church, not even for her son's baptism. It was humbling, this business of moving into people's lives. They had families and relationships. A complicated web. Shift one strand and everything was affected.

I noticed Freddy moving his eyes in her direction several times. Finally, I realized he was signalling me to talk with his mother and invite her to the women's meeting that I was on my way to that very afternoon.

I chatted with her for a few minutes and then said, "I was just on my way to a meeting for women. Would you like to come with me?"

"I think so. Yes, okay, I'll come. But I have to *arreglar* first."

She went off to change her dress and fix her hair. By this time about seven young kids had gathered in the patio so I sat down on an old chair in the corner to wait for her and to watch Martin and Freddy teach the kids' club.

Freddy came up to me, a worried look on his face. "Are you staying?"

"Sure," I said.

"Well," he said in a whisper with his hand on my shoulder, "the truth is that just today we are not very well prepared and—"

"Well," I laughed, "then for sure I'll stay. Part of being a good teacher is knowing how to improvise!"

The children were soon engaged in songs and activity. I was satisfied to see the youth relating well to the children.

As I waited the time moved past 2:30 p.m., the start time of the women's meeting. I told myself – *patience – you're in Latin America now.* I had not yet learned the lesson that the Colombians knew much better than I, a supposed leader. I was usually intent on gearing up for the next thing, while they valued the present moment. This meant they were appreciative of the little things in life. I tended to be goal-oriented, focusing on the next event rather than the present one.

When Freddy's mother finally emerged in a pretty pastel dress with her hair in a tidy bun, a married sister of Freddy's walked into the room with her and asked to come along to the meeting as well. As we walked down the street I felt very happy to have them with me but I was worried about the time.

"I'm sorry that I'm bringing you late to this meeting when you are coming for the first time. You'll miss part of the activities."

They shrugged, "No *importa*."

We three women walked into the meeting thirty-five minutes after the planned start time. To my surprise the meeting was just getting started. People were going around the circle introducing each other. I learned to love that about Latin America! Time was elastic. And when those coloured cups of *tinto* were placed in their hands, Freddy's mother and sister soon felt they could belong in our community.

15   Surprises for our visitors

Seven months after we moved to Medellín we had visitors from Winnipeg who boosted our morale. My father, John M. Schmidt, my sister Shirley and her daughter Maria arrived laden with gifts and news from home. They joined our church meetings, they bumped along in our jeep up to a shantytown to visit church members, and we took a few days to vacation at a hotel down the mountain.

I wondered what my preacher father would think of how we were handling the work of a pastor, the work of the curing of souls. After a Sunday morning service in which the people responded with sincere prayers, he told Harold and me, "Your mother and I are very proud of the work you're doing here." His words put a smile on my face.

Rebecca turns 10 years old. Next to me is my sister Shirley, Conrad, my dad, Andy and Maria.

My dad and Shirley were shocked, though, at the poverty, the crime and the effect of the drug lords on Medellín. We made sure not to tell them certain things. For instance, one day I planned for us to go shopping at Exito in the barrio of Poblado. That morning the paper reported a major confrontation the previous day in Poblado between the military and the guerrillas. I decided to say nothing. We went off with our visitors and we enjoyed a carefree day of shopping. No incident marred the day and once back home I breathed a sigh of relief.

One day a six-year-old girl from the church invited Rebecca and Maria to her birthday party. We had them dress in their Sunday best and dropped them off at the home, a humble home near the church. When we picked them up again, they each held a small box. The boxes emitted strange noises.

"Look what we got! Look!"

Inside were live baby chicks.

"What in the world—"

"What are we going to do with those?"

At home, the only place we could find to safely keep them was in a shower stall.

"Why would they get a live chick as a party favor?" asked my dad.

"It can mean a great deal to a family. They would feed it and keep it and eventually have eggs or eat the bird. We'll give these away to a family that will really appreciate them."

One day we toured the open meat market with its pungent smells and aproned butchers axing beef quarters on tree stumps, wood chips flying. I bought racks of spareribs there which I planned for supper the next day. Because I would be away at a women's meeting during the afternoon, I asked Shirley to cut up the ribs and put them in the oven.

At 4:40 I returned home from the women's meeting. What was this? Shirley, an award-winning pianist, playing piano. Matthew in the kitchen cutting up ribs. They greeted my puzzled looks with laughter.

"Oh, after the smells in that meat market yesterday I couldn't face touching those ribs," Shirley confessed. "I just couldn't. I bribed Matthew into chopping them up. But I'm valiantly supporting him. Listen — " She launched into the hymn, "Toil on, toil on." Then a few bars of "Work for the night is coming."

Oh, did we laugh!

At suppertime Harold and Dad walked in the door. Dad looked tired as he took off his hat and placed it on the shelf by the door.

Matthew with spareribs. Toil on!

"Where have you two been?"

"Out at banks," my dad said. "I have travelers' cheques to cash but it's a no go."

"Went to three banks," Harold sighed. "No one will cash travelers' cheques in this city. Against the law."

"To cut down on money laundering, they say. Won't even exchange the American dollars I brought for pesos. "

"Oh, I'm sorry. We didn't know. You can borrow pesos from us while you're here."

"But that's just what I don't want," my dad said, "I want to give you money, not take from you."

"It's only for a while…."

"I'll put it back in your account in Canada the first day back in Winnipeg."

"Let's eat! We have spare ribs."

The ribs were delicious in a homemade barbecue sauce, a recipe from a Texan missionary at language school in Costa Rica. Shirley good-naturedly took the teasing for not tasting the ribs.

My dad, who was usually fussy about what he ate, announced, "I want to take us adults out for a special meal. You choose where. Some place really nice."

Shirley, my dad and Harold. This restaurant was damaged the next day by a car bomb attack.

One of their last evenings in Medellín, we four adults went out to eat. We chose a tipico restaurant across the road from the Hotel

Intercontinental with a Colombian menu aimed to please tourists. Seated outdoors under a thatched roof patio we enjoyed a delicious meal that included roast beef called muchacho and one of my favorites, humble but delicious patacones, fried plantain.

The next day the news' headlines showed that a car bomb exploded on that road. That very restaurant was damaged! That news helped our guests to be a little less regretful when they bid us farewell at the airport.

My heart sank to see them go. "I miss you already!" I called as they walked away.

16 The doctor who wasn't and the other guy who was

Cough, cough, cough! This was a common sound in our home. Me coughing. Ever since the final semester of studies in Costa Rica, I had been plagued with a cough. I didn't know the cause. In Medellín I continued to cough and cough, one bronchial infection after another and constantly on the hunt for medicine that would cure me.

I made an appointment with an Ear, Nose and Throat specialist downtown on the ground floor of a modern building. I felt assured by the affluent surroundings that here was a successful doctor. It never crossed my mind that it could be a front.

A secretary buzzed me in through the double glass doors. I stepped into an immense reception room, a sanctuary that was high-ceilinged, richly carpeted and furnished with polished mahogany pieces. I felt I should curtsy, not be waited on. Passing the reception area, I was shown into the examination room. What a room.

Later I told Harold, "That room could hold four of our living rooms, it was that huge! And I had to wade across an acre of thick carpet to reach the chair to sit in."

The doctor, seated behind a massive mahogany desk, smiled at me. He asked my symptoms and his plump hand duly noted them in a file folder. Meanwhile my eyes scanned the room. There was no indication of medical supplies anywhere. But along one side of the room seven antique wooden tables lined the wall. On each one rested an antique optometric contrivance no longer in use, painted black.

The doctor followed my gaze and explained in a conspiratorial whisper, "I collect antiques."

Then he pointed to an antique barber chair in red leather in a far corner near the back wall. He motioned me to that chair and I walked over to climb into it. Meanwhile he shuffled back a quarter mile across the carpet and disappeared into an adjoining room.

When he emerged, in one hand he carried a fat little glass bottle topped with a wick that reminded me of high school chemistry class. His other hand was down by his side, hiding something. He held the Bunsen burner up close to my face. Then his other hand swept over it and, like a magic trick, a great flame leaped out inches from my eyes.

I recoiled, throwing myself against the back of the chair.

"No, no, my dear, it is nothing." He chuckled at his little joke and placed the burner on a tray next to the chair. "It is only to warm up the instruments so that the cold does not shock you."

He waved the metal tongue depressor over the flame and then had me say, "Ah-h-h." Later the ear instrument was also duly heated. Then he prescribed a medication.

It didn't help.

I wrote in my journal, "I feel discouraged. Still sick since coming to Medellín and I just get worse. Been coughing all week. This noon we had an elder from the Colombian national conference and his wife over for lunch. They stayed till 3 p.m. I coughed and coughed and couldn't breathe, etc. Very bad. This happens over and over. Am sore from coughing. What does the Lord have for me? Right now, it seems my job is to continue to live joyfully regardless of circumstances."

Over the next months, that doctor followed the same procedure in each consultation. Always the little Bunsen burner played the lead role with the tongue depressor and ear instrument taking supporting roles. I saw no evidence of other medical equipment. He never took blood pressure or temperature. And, invariably, regardless of symptoms, he prescribed the same antibiotic.

Many times I carried his prescription to the drugstore closest to our house where a young woman pointed me into a tiny not-very-clean washroom piled to the ceiling with boxes. She pushed the door half closed, told me to remove my belt, pulled my waistband down and injected an antibiotic into my hip.

It didn't help.

"You must move to another city," the doctor said. "Medellín is not good for you. The industries, the buses, the traffic. All bad."

"Our work is here, I can't just move somewhere else."

"Can't you go back to Canada for a few months to recuperate?"

I shook my head.

"Well, then you must go away to the countryside each weekend to give your lungs a rest."

Haha. Church work revolves around weekends.

At home I was becoming distressed.

"What's wrong with me?" I asked Harold. "I'm so tired of this. I've been sick for more than a year now. Every time I'm so hopeful the new medication will help, but then it doesn't. I feel so guilty."

"Guilty? For what?"

"Don't you think something is wrong with me? There must be something I've done wrong to be sick so much. Could it be a spiritual problem?"

"You can't feel guilty for being sick. You can't control it. It makes no sense to feel guilty."

"Not to you. You haven't been sick," I grumbled.

Thinking we might have to move to some other city or another country disturbed me. I couldn't face the idea and refused to discuss such a move even with Harold.

My own mother had been ill most of her life. I usually saw her lying in bed. Sometimes she was away in hospital and we kids were farmed out to other families. The idea of being ill filled me with dread. My dream was to be successful like my pastor father, not plagued by ill health as my mother had been. I poured out my frustration in my journal.

"It all smells of failure. I can't face it. I was prepared to meet the challenge of living and working here in Medellín no matter how violent. How ironic if, instead of violence or danger sending us away, it could simply be air pollution!"

One afternoon when the diagnosis and prescription were dittoes again, I ventured to ask the doctor. "Is it normal to have the same cough, the same infection month after month? Maybe we could do other tests like an X-ray? Maybe ask another doctor for an opinion?"

"But my dear lady," his voice quavered in shocked hurt. "Other doctors cannot help you more than I can. I am the specialist for exactly your problem. Do you not trust me? Trust me. I know what I'm doing. There is much we haven't tried yet. Yes, yes, on the next visit we will begin a different line altogether."

I didn't go back.

Instead, I found the name and address of an allergy specialist. To reach him I had to climb up three flights of narrow stairs in a dull downtown building to find his office comprised of three tiny, cramped rooms.

He was tall, thin, with thick glasses topped by a bunch of surprised looking hair. It was obvious from the start that what captivated him were bugs. His walls were covered with posters of enormous bugs and he delighted in pointing them out with all their nasty features. I felt he had no interest in me, only in bugs.

I liked him immediately.

He became engrossed in the mystery of which of those bugs was the one plaguing my respiratory system. Many questions, many scribbled notes. Then, when I asked a question about those bugs, he leaped from his chair in ecstasy, "I'll show you!"

Dragging me from the room, he rushed me into a tiny lab. A semi-dressed woman in a chair sat with one arm extended on a table. The poor woman reached for a sheet to cover her shoulders. He took no notice of her fright but took hold of her arm and pointed to rows of red dots, allergy pricks he had made all the way from shoulder to wrist.

"This one, ho!" Pointing at the red dots, he declared, "This definitely, yes, is something. See the bump?"

He had eyes only for bugs. After Ear, Nose and Antiques, I could have hugged him. He explained that in Medellín the diesel fumes from vehicles and the smoke from industry stayed trapped in the valley giving the city's inhabitants an unusually high rate of lung disease. The number of children with recurring respiratory infections was exceptionally high.

Under his care I began to get well immediately. I wrote to my parents, "After just five days on these new medications I rarely cough and I don't get bronchial spasms. It's like night and day! I feel like a new person.

"He says my bronchia have been inflamed for more than a year now and I have intrinsic asthma. He put me on this treatment for a few months, sprays and tablets. For the first time in months I can sleep through the night. I'm so thankful."

When all the tests were back, the doctor concluded a number of allergens had affected my lungs. Even if I returned to Manitoba, I might be no better off, given the soil and grain dust on the prairies.

I wrote home, "Thank God it looks like we can stay on here in Medellín. There are so many exciting developments in the church work that we don't want to leave."

I told my new doctor what my past treatment had been with Ear, Nose and Antiques. He exclaimed, "No, no! Impossible, absolutely impossible. That was no doctor."

17   Fumbling through a funeral

Homicide was the leading cause of death for adult males in Colombia. But the first funeral we experienced first-hand was not a homicide. It was Benji.

Just a few months after we started work in Medellin, Harold arrived home with news, "I saw Benji in the hospital."

"How'd you manage that?" I asked. "How'd you get in?"

Harold had tried before but it was impossible. Two armed guards stood at the locked entrance to the social security hospital. At the start of visiting hours, they opened the door a crack to let in card-bearers one by one. Only those with a visitor's card were allowed in. The card-bearers, usually family members, assembled in lines outside that sometimes stretched for blocks. Only two visitor cards per patient were issued. Since Benji had a huge extended family, his cards were always taken.

"So how did you get in this time?" I asked.

"Waited outside the emergency entrance. Pretty soon a bad case arrived. Three people with gunshot wounds. Lots of screaming relatives. I slipped in with them. Then I walked around until I found the right ward."

"Ah, I kinda wondered why you were all spiffed up in a suit and tie today. Was it bad in there?"

"Terrible. Like a M.A.S.H. unit. Blood all over the place. Three people on wooden stretchers crying for attention, blood running down the floor. Doctors get a lot of practice in this city."

Benji was a soft-spoken twenty-year-old who dreamed of becoming a singer. After church Sunday evenings he often shyly called Harold aside and demonstrated what he had learned on the guitar that week. Sometimes he sang a composition of his own.

When he came down with a fever, the doctor found a tumor on his spine. He was admitted to the social security hospital to have it removed. Benji woke from his surgery to find himself paralyzed from the waist down. The surgeon's knife had cut too deeply. But for poor people there was no compensation and definitely no thought of a lawsuit. They shrugged and said God must have willed it.

For a few months his mother cared for him along with the other eight children in their third-floor apartment. One warm April evening Benji slipped away.

We suddenly found ourselves in charge of planning a funeral that had to take place within twenty-four hours of death. Since we had not yet even attended a funeral in Colombia, we had no idea of funeral protocol.

The evening Benji died, Harold spent the night with the family arranging funeral details, drinking lots of cups of *tinto* between the tears.

In the morning, Galen and Linda and I ordered an immense basket of white lilies and burgundy roses. Galen offered to look after some other details, Linda took Conrad to their house for the morning and I took a taxi to be with the mother, Silvia.

On the sidewalk in front of the building where she and her children lived stood a large white card leaning against the concrete step announcing the funeral for three o'clock that afternoon.

The house was narrow, four storeys tall. On each level lived a different family, all related to each other. The façade was zigzagged with concrete stairways ending at the entrance to each level. As I climbed up, on each landing I passed relatives dressed in black, whispering in little huddles.

Through the open door of the third-floor apartment, I saw the plain wooden coffin on its metal stand, set diagonally across the tiny *sala*.

Silvia came to greet me. After we hugged she led me to the coffin. I had a fierce admiration for this woman who had lived all her married life in this apartment raising her nine children. She was the most serene and contented woman I knew. And yet she put up with an unfaithful husband who drank, lived with a mistress and showed up at home whenever he needed his clothes washed.

Because the poor do not embalm their dead, the coffin was sealed shut with only a small glass window over the head for viewing the face of the departed. We gazed in silence, trying to ignore a drunken uncle who kept putting his face next to the glass drooling over it as great sobs shook his body.

I sat down to join other women who circled the room seated in plain wooden chairs. All wore black dresses, black stockings and black shoes. All moaned and lifted wet hankies to their eyes. I too had dressed carefully in subdued tones.

But Silvia defied tradition and family expectations. She wore a pure white cotton dress with white flats on her feet! And in that room of weeping relatives she sat composed, an island of calm, her face peaceful. Contrary to traditional beliefs, she was convinced that Benji had arrived safely in heaven. She announced her belief with her clothes and her serenity.

I admired her nerve. I was too new to the culture to realize that her action did not inspire admiration in others as it did in me.

Self-composure and being strong in your grief are not admired traits among Colombians. Rather, an outpouring of emotion and great grief is the expected expression of love.

Since Harold and I were the church leaders, we arrived early at the church rented for the occasion. Our own church would not have held the expected crowds. In the hot afternoon it was refreshingly cool under the high tin roof. No ushers had been assigned so people moved into whatever pews they chose. I hurried to reserve the two front benches for Silvia and her family. Then I chose a seat for Conrad and myself. Other benches filled up and soon there were people standing, lining the walls and the back of the church.

A hearse brought the coffin to the church. Six female attendants rolled it down the aisle. They were dressed in uniforms, black cloaks and black pillbox hats, their faces set in stony impassivity. Crows, I thought. For them it was just another day of business in funeral-ridden Medellín. No, I wanted to scream, it's not, it's not. It's Benji!

Behind the coffin, in straggled formation came the family. The thin, unfaithful husband had his arm around plump little Silvia, resplendent in her white dress. The eight children followed, aged two to twenty-one.

After settling the coffin in its place, the Crows, who had numerous funerals every day, marched back down the aisle to wait outdoors. I expected the family to take their seats in the front benches I had saved for them. But they stayed standing in the aisle behind the coffin. Didn't they know what to do next? They must be waiting for an indication from someone.

Slipping out of my seat I laid my hand on Silvia's shoulder and whispered, "Please sit down. There's room for all of you right here."

She turned questioningly to her husband.

"No, no. That's fine," said the husband. "We'll stand."

I went back to my seat. The whole family stayed standing in the aisle. Finally, the speaker stood to give a sermon. I'd never known this man to speak less than forty minutes and I was convinced that Silvia couldn't last on her feet. She'd been up all night.

Once again, I got up from my place in the packed church and whispered, "Won't you sit down? This will take a long time, yet."

"No," the husband firmly stated, his eyes narrowing. "*Somos personas muy de pi*e. We are standing-type people."

Chagrined, I returned to my place. Suddenly a familiar uneasiness swept over me. Why was I, the foreigner, concerning myself with that which apparently everyone else was accepting? Did everyone in this crowd know something I didn't know? Why hadn't I just relaxed instead of making a fool of myself, jumping up several times?

Only later I discovered that the husband, a Catholic, had not wanted to contaminate himself by sitting down in a Protestant church. Someone could report him to the priest and he would be in trouble. Standing had been his silent protest and his family had had to fall in line. Everyone else understood.

Exactly one hour into the service, while Benji's brother was speaking a eulogy, the Crows marched back down the aisle, their faces stern. They took hold of the coffin and wheeled it down the aisle and outside to the waiting hearse. Their contract said one hour and one hour was up.

Seeing them come for the coffin, the crowd ignored what was happening on the platform and poured out into the street and into the buses rented for the occasion. We filled our jeep with people and followed down the long highway to the graveyard.

There, Harold parked the jeep, took his Bible in hand and walked up the hill planning to give a short graveside service. But as we came over the hill to the open grave, we saw the Crows had reached it ahead of us. They were already lowering the coffin into the ground.

"What are they doing?" I cried. "How dare they? They act like they're in charge of the whole funeral!"

But before we could reach them, the six of them practically threw the coffin into the grave, ran down the hill to the hearse and sped off to their next engagement. That was it. No ceremony, no respectful silence. Death was an assembly-line production in Medellín.

Now the relatives gathered at the brink of the grave wailing loudly and extending their arms into the space over the grave as if hoping to draw Benji up to themselves again.

"What do we do now?" I asked, turning to Harold.

"No use trying to read Scripture in this noise," he said. "Where's Guillermo with the guitar?"

Guillermo strummed a few opening chords. The church people began to sing. As their singing gathered momentum, the wailing of the relatives and neighbours slowly waned. They stared and listened.

We sang with all our might.

"*Que gloriosa la mañana…* How glorious that morning will be!"

"*El es mi paz…* Jesus is my peace and has removed all my fears."

We bewildered those who, until then, had seen wailing as the only response at a graveside. But we sang from our hearts for Benji, and most of all for Silvia, quietly composed, her white shoes touching the graveside, her face smiling through the tears.

18   Pieces of the puzzle

One thing we didn't need in Colombia was an alarm clock. At 6:15 every morning the churches rang their bells for early mass. The nearest one was one hundred yards from our house. Then by 6:30 we heard several young men passing our windows shouting in a singsong voice, *"El Colombiano! El Espectador!"* The morning paper had arrived.

Twice a week by 6:45 we heard a steadily honking horn coming ever closer. Ah yes, garbage day, *basura*. In case anyone was hearing impaired, a huge bell hung from the front bumper of the garbage truck. Every few houses, this bell was vigorously clanged along with the honking horn. That brought the *señoras* and maids onto their front steps with the garbage cans they had dragged through the house from the back patio. There were no back lanes in Colombia.

Then, in case anyone missed all the racket, the garbage men continually called out at the top of their voices, *"Basura! Basura!"* It was like a grand parade passing slowly by.

In spite of the early start to the day, Colombian Christians often held prayer vigils late into the night. I learned to enjoy these occasions. A sweet unity emerged between church members as we sang chorus after chorus, then prayed for hours. Even in a six-hour *vigilia*, time flew by!

But, oh the tension I felt between throwing myself fully into church work and caring for the family. I would usually resolve it by leaving early, asking one of the young men to run out to hail a taxi for me around 9 p.m., then hurrying home to make sure the kids were in bed for the next day's school.

A main challenge for Harold and me was knowing what to say in each new setting and each home we visited. One week a tall, earnest man called Hernando visited the church, met Harold and begged us to come to his house.

"Please, I have many, many questions. And our baby is sick and we need you to offer prayers for her. Will you come?"

We had already met with different people throughout that day but we decided we needed to visit Hernando that evening. We found his house in a very poor barrio, pushed into the mountainside. Could it be called a house or was it a cave? The doorway was so low we had to bend to go through. Hernando led us through a narrow entry into the main room that served as living room, kitchen and bedroom. As we passed through the entryway, we squeezed by a narrow bed on which two children were asleep, one at the head and the other at the foot, making room for both to sleep.

Our hearts went out to this man and his family and we tried to offer words of hope. Harold and I fell silent on our drive home, reflecting on the starkness of that home and the gratitude the family had expressed for our visit. It always surprised me to find people's faith and hope in the darkest corners. Even in the midst of squalor there was a note of tenderness and sometimes almost an ironic smile that said, *Look what's become of us.*

A few days later I was scheduled to give a talk to the church youth group.

"We need a talk on how to date in a Christian way. Will you please come and speak at our meeting?"

So, there I was. There was no Internet, of course, and few resources, so my ideas came from my own experience and from biographies and self-help books I'd read. A number of new young people were there, some from other churches. As I spoke, Belinda, one of our church teens, began to cry. She cried throughout, likely because I warned against dating unbelieving boyfriends. That was what she was doing, against her parents' wishes.

After my talk, I met a beautiful fourteen-year-old girl who attended a different church. She asked if she could talk with me in private. We sat down together in a Sunday School classroom.

"*Señora* Doroti, something bad happened to me. I take the public bus to school every day and last week I noticed that these two men followed me a few times. Then those men tried to talk to me. I didn't want to talk with them."

She started to sob. But she soon composed herself and eventually the story came out. Both men had raped her and she was now going to have to testify against them.

My heart dropped. Tears came to my eyes.

"I am so grateful that I wasn't killed," she said.

What sort of lives do these people live, I wondered silently, where to survive a crime is seen as a success? I counselled her as best I could and prayed with her.

"Now, how can I help you?" I asked. "I can come to court with you if I know what day."

"No! No! My mother and my aunts have forbidden me to tell anyone. No one must know. My mother says it must be my own fault. She is so ashamed."

That wrenched my heart.

"So please," she begged me, "please do not tell anyone that I told you. I would get into big troubles, much bigger than what has already happened."

My heart sank. What should I do? I gave her a card with my number.

"Please call me anytime. Anytime at all, okay? And I'll pray that God's angels guard you." Yes, I said that, even though I realized how irrelevant it must sound to her—where were the angels when she needed them?

I went home sad, thinking *Every person we know has pain and urgent needs in their life and it seems we can do so little to help.*

Trevor and Joan Godard with their boys,
Silas and Aaron.

Then, just when we needed a lift, our good friends Trever and Joan Godard, now working in Cali, stopped by. They came from visiting the coastal churches in the Chocó, and were stopping in Medellín before flying the next day back to Cali. Our spirits soared when they said they could stay until the next day. They walked in the door looking tired, and collapsed on the sofa.

"We're all tuckered out. It's stifling hot and humid at the coast and we were stuck sixteen hours traveling in a Chiva bus."

"Sixteen hours! So, you just want to get to sleep?"

"No way!" They stayed up with us past midnight sharing their stories and listening as we told our adventures and challenges. It was a brief stopover but it fed our spirits and injected us with new courage.

That week was a typical week for us, visiting a different home each day, counselling a married woman having an affair, visiting the sick and new attenders to the church. One evening a young female university student, our neighbour, popped over to ask our help in translating an English text. I was very tired and wished I could relax after a full day. But we invited her in, thinking it would be a brief visit. She stayed two hours.

The next morning I really wanted to rest. But I had promised Valeria, an older woman new to our church, that I would come to talk with her. So off I went, though I took a taxi that day instead of fighting with buses. Valeria received me graciously and thanked me for coming to answer her questions.

"I don't know why my family has suddenly turned cold. We were so close before. Especially my grown-up son and daughter. I tell them they should come to the meetings with me. I leave the leaflets from the church on the table so they will read them. I pray out loud so they will hear what a prayer should be like. Now they hardly speak to me."

Usually we didn't need to tell people to hold off, but Valeria was pushing religion down her family's throat and making them hate the church that she loved, the opposite effect she hoped for. As kindly as I could I explained this to her. Poor woman. She was sincere but misguided. When I left I was not sure she was going to change at all.

 ## 19　Off to join the army

Harold and I were on our way to visit a young man, Santiago, and his mother Lucia who faithfully attended our church. Santiago was leaving the next day to report for his compulsory military duty.

Colombian families dreaded the day their sons were forced into the army. In their final year of high school, all Colombian young men were required to report to military headquarters. Not all were put into service. By pulling lots it was decided which ones actually had to serve the required eighteen months in the military. Well-to-do parents with money for bribes could get their sons exempt, but the vast masses of poor did not have that option. Of those who were chosen, every mother's wish was for her son to be assigned a post in the city, not out in the mountains and villages facing the guerrilla armies.

When we first arrived in Colombia, the sight of guns and soldiers in the streets jarred me. Very quickly I got used to military roadblocks, seeing them as just a nuisance, like rush hour traffic. I got used to hearing gunshots or seeing guards or soldiers with rifles guarding the shops and banks.

I got used to seeing soldiers on the street.

Police were permitted to stop any young men on the road at any time and demand to see their *tarjeta*. If they did not carry their military card stating they had either served or been exempt, they could be tossed up into the back of a truck and carried off. I had seen this happen.

Driving on our way to the farewell meeting with Santiago, I thought back to our first encounter with soldiers a few weeks after our arrival in Colombia.

Harold and I were in the jeep on our way up a mountainside to the home of a church member who was ill. A large green sign across the road read *RETEN MILITAR*. Soldiers in battle fatigues lined both sides of the highway, rifles at the ready. As the jeep slowed, my heart rate sped up. This was the first military roadblock we'd ever encountered. What would they do with us? Would they treat us badly for being foreigners?

As we pulled to a stop, two soldiers approached us, one leaned in at Harold's open window and the other at mine.

"Documentos por favor."

From his shirt pocket Harold surrendered several cards and papers.

"You have no driver's licence."

"This is my Canadian licence. We've only been in Colombia a short time. We'll soon have a Colombian licence."

I tensed.

Then the soldier on my side, hooking his rifle belt over his shoulder, craned his neck in at my window.

"Abre el cajón," he told me.

"Como?" What did he want? I understood the word "Open" but I couldn't understand what he wanted opened.

"Abre el cajón!"

He must want to check my purse. Nervously I placed my purse under his nose and pulled open the zipper. He glanced down, then across to his partner at the other window. A slight shake of the head and then a slow grin spread across his face.

He's only a kid! I realized. Maybe eighteen, no more, he had a wide brown face with amused eyes. My tension died away and a wry grin crept over my face.

Slowly, I shook my head, *"Perdón señor,* I just don't know what you're saying."

His hand reached in the window to tap the glove compartment. *"Esto."*

"Ahhh." *Cajón*. Glove compartment. Another Spanish word learned the hard way.

After that first experience, military roadblocks soon became part of everyday life, usually following the same pattern. The men in the vehicle had to get out, were leaned against the vehicle and frisked from top to toe. Women had their bags searched and documents checked. Children were ignored. No matter how many times we were stopped, the *retén* always made us groan and mutter, "Not this again."

Now we would be bidding farewell to Santiago, a teenager soon to be dressed in battle fatigues. We parked in a vast guarded lot and looked around. It was a fairly new housing development of ghetto dwellings, row housing. All around us thousands of concrete boxes climbed up the hillside in tiers, like rows of seats in a stadium. Five tiers. Each tier held a street of concrete boxes. There were no front yards. Every door opened directly onto a central concrete walkway. These concrete homes were so tiny that the three geraniums planted by Lucia's door took up all the space between her door and the common wall that separated her house from the neighbours.

"How are you, *hermana*?" She greeted me in the traditional way. Lucia was tall, with the face of a beauty queen and a serene manner. We walked through the traditional greetings.

"We are well, thank you sister," I answered. "And you?"

"We are sad, thank you. And what can you tell me?"

"My family is all well, thank you. And your family?"

"Nothing new, *gracias*, only that they are robbing me of my son."

"Mama!" called Santiago, appearing in the *sala*. "I'll be back home very soon."

Following the Colombian custom, Lucia showed me around all

the rooms of the house. Her husband had disappeared and Lucia lived here with her six children. Two tiny bedrooms, a kitchen and the *sala* that held the couch as well as the family dining table.

She supported her family by selling empanadas and yucca rolls that she made on the gray concrete counter in the tiny kitchen. She pointed out to me where each child slept. The table they ate at during the day became at night the bed for the ten-year-old. Next to the table was the narrow couch where the youngest spent the night. It was a better-furnished house than most in the ghettos. Besides the couch it had an armchair of ancient flocked velvet, well worn.

She pointed to the velvet chair for Harold and the couch for me. She brought us each a deep bowl of hot chocolate and a *pan de yuca*, a chewy roll made from the root of the cassava plant. One of my favourites!

Santiago leaned forward on a wooden chair and spoke shyly about going off to the army. While Lucia struggled to hold back tears, I saw he was working to quell the air of excitement he felt at this new adventure.

"I've packed a Bible," he told us proudly.

"Where you're going it'll be difficult to read it. Others will make fun of you," Harold said.

"*Sí, hermano*. I know."

"You're leaving your friends and your family behind but God will go with you. So keep talking with him. You'll stay strong reading your Bible and talking with God."

"Si, hermano, I know this. What you say is the truth."

They asked us to pray. After prayers, Lucia wiped her eyes with a handkerchief and they walked a short way with us toward our jeep. We hugged them goodbye, the mother tearful, the son already living in the venture that would start the next day.

Two months later Lucia called me from the ghetto's communal payphone as they had no phone of their own.

"*Hermana*, something happened. A young man, a nice man, came to my door. He asks, 'Is your son Santiago?' And I say, 'Yes.'

"'Is your son in such and such a division and in such and such a place?' I say, 'I think so.' Then he says, 'I'm also from there and I'm returning tomorrow. If you would like to send a package to your son I'll take it to him.'

"And so, *hermana*, I made a small package. I put in something special from the house and I put in all the money that I didn't need for rice and beans for the children that week.

"But now it's a long time since he was here and I haven't heard that my son got this package. And now my neighbours tell me that they've heard of other mothers who also were robbed in this way. Oh, why do they make us suffer so much—we mothers who are already in pain?"

After her call I held the receiver in my hand for a long time. That was the question for so much that happened in Colombia. *Why?*

And I was the last person qualified to answer that. Our three sons had been born in Canada and would never be required to join the country's armed forces.

Colombia's famous writer, Gabriel Garcia Marquez, was heard to say on his death bed, "My God, if I had a heart, I would engrave my hatred on a block of ice and wait for the sun to come out."

Everyone was waiting—when would the sun come out over Colombia?

20 In which I am, yet again, an ignorant foreigner

The first time I held a bottle of red wine was on an Avianca plane from Miami to Medellín. Thirty-five years old with no knowledge of alcoholic drinks. At that time in our lives, we were complete abstainers. I had never touched alcohol nor had ever had any in the house. A good Mennonite Brethren girl.

In Medellín my challenge came not only from switching to the Colombian from the Canadian culture but from adapting to society outside the insular one in which I had grown up. Within the Mennonite milieu our social gatherings were quite different from social events in other groups but I had not learned that yet when at thirty-five years old I arrived in Colombia.

On that flight a savoury aroma of beef filled the air, followed by smiling stewardesses handing out dinner trays. Every passenger, even in economy class, received a full steak dinner. And on each tray lay a small bottle of red wine.

Of course, we had no thought of opening the bottles but to leave these bottles on the tray unopened seemed a sad waste. We Mennonites are proud of our thrift. At the end of our row I saw a Colombian man open his bottle and pour.

"Harold," I said, "Let's pass our bottles to that guy. He can take them home."

We did.

The man's narrow eyes opened wide. *"Gracias!"*

The children followed suit. They picked up the small bottles by their thumbs and fingertips as though handling vials of poison and passed them gingerly down the row.

"Gracias, gracias!" Our new friend bobbed his head, *"Gracias!"* as he opened one bottle after the other.

"Oh dear," I whispered. "He's not saving them for home." As he drank he grew more and more amiable, his reddening face nodding up and down.

"Oh well," I shrugged and returned his smile. We had, after all, come to Colombia to spread cheer.

Our abstinence from social drinking was one feature that stood at odds with the culture. It was not a problem, though, with our church people. They wrote off any difference in behaviour or speech as what one could expect from the role of missionary.

During our first year in Medellín I felt I learned a lot about how Colombians eat. But I still knew so little.

"I would like you to come for lunch to my house," Elsa said one day. This was the Elsa with whom I walked through the shootout near the church. Her husband drank away much of their income so I marvelled that she offered me a meal.

"If you bring the meat," she added, "I will make everything else."

"What kind of meat?"

"It doesn't matter. Whatever you like."

That didn't help.

When the day came, I took the bus to a grocery store and looked over the meat selection. I just could not understand what sort of meat could be prepared on the spot after I walked in the door for lunch. I was thinking very Canadian—that you walk in and lunch is ready to be served. So, I chose a good-sized ham piece that would not need to be cooked. Then, wanting to bring a treat, I added a bag of cream-filled cookies.

Because the way to Elsa's home was complicated, I flagged a taxi. The winding streets became ever narrower and more crowded with people and bicycles as we climbed the hill. I was deposited in a ghetto parking lot. Circling the lot in every direction were layers of houses connected by concrete stairways, much like Lucia's house.

Beyond the first flight of stairs leading up from the parking lot rose another level of stairways and then above them more stairways and then still more, like the inside of some gigantic stadium. At each level were built a line of houses, concrete boxes in long rows - the houses of the working poor. How many thousands lived in this one complex?

After finding the correct section number, up I went, one flight, then another, then a third and fourth. How did Elsa drag her drunk husband up to their house on a Friday evening?

Elsa stood waiting outside her door. On a patch of dusty earth between the rows of houses a handful of children were kicking a soccer ball around with little enthusiasm. Her house of unpainted concrete blocks looked exactly like all the others. But Elsa had painted her door a happy apple green.

"Please come in. It's wonderful you could come!" Elsa hugged me and drew me in. Inside the door in the tiny *sala* were two webbed lawn chairs, the only furniture.

"Come and see the house. *Conocer la casa*," she invited. She immediately showed me around the house so that I could relax, ruling out danger from eavesdroppers or knife-wielding enemies. There were two tiny bedrooms with no closets and just enough space to walk between the beds. The bathroom had a curtain for a door and the showerhead stuck out of the wall between the toilet and the sink. The whole room would become a shower stall each time anyone showered.

She invited me to sit down in the *sala* on the lawn chair from where I could watch her at the stove in the cubbyhole kitchen. We could chat as she cooked.

She put black beans in a pressure cooker and as I watched it dawned on me that she must have been hoping for a nice cut of red beef that would have cooked in minutes and given rich flavour to the beans in that pressure cooker.

Of course! All Colombians in Medellín use pressure cookers. Otherwise at the altitude of five thousand feet, beans would take hours to cook. I must have been the sole homemaker with no pressure cooker, too scared to use one. To me it was a noisy steaming dragon threatening to explode and tear through the roof.

Elsa showed no disappointment with the ham and added it in after the beans had cooked. She handed me a plate with this mixture, which was delicious. With the beans came a heaping mound of white rice and a tasty salad of tomatoes and onions.

She did not serve herself but only sat and watched me eat. I knew the pot of food was the main meal for her sons and husband and she would portion it out for each of them. No doubt she did not want me to see how small her own portion would be compared to what she served me.

Colombia is full of brave, strong, persevering and self-sacrificing women like Elsa. I so admire them!

After I'd eaten, while we were drinking *tinto*, her youngest son, ten-year-old Geraldo, came home from school. By some unspoken message he did not even ask about lunch which mothers always give their children when they come home from school, usually between one and two o'clock. He was waiting until I left so that I would not see that my portion had been, likely, about twice what the members of the family ate.

None of them were robust. During my visit Elsa told me how the doctor had said to give vitamins to this youngest son who was in poor health. But, of course, she couldn't afford such luxury.

Oh, how silly I felt for bringing those useless cream cookies for dessert. Why hadn't I brought fruit, which was likely, a rare treat and just what they needed for good health! But no, I had been thinking like a rich, well-fed North American with the luxury to bypass fruit and reach for a cream cookie. Though I didn't deserve it, Elsa seemed to love me anyway.

21 Taste of death with a side of soup

Up twisting concrete stairs, past an old man hunched on a step in a worn trench coat smoking a cigarette. Harold and I were on our way to visit Alicia, a fifty-year-old woman who had recently joined our church.

We saw Alicia, dressed in a loose cotton print dress outside her adobe brick house with her metal front door ajar. Waiting for us, I thought.

But no. She stood peering away from us toward a knot of people gathered across the street in front of a small corner storefront, the local *tienda*.

She turned as we approached. "Oh, Arold y Doroti, I did not see you come up! Just now our storekeeper was shot." She pointed. I looked more closely at the scene across the street and saw that at the centre of the group lay a man on the sidewalk.

"Oh no! What happened?"

"Like always," she shrugged. "A motorcycle came by with two men. They slowed down, shot the man and drove away fast. He died right away, poor man."

I knew the papers reported at least ten murders a day in Medellín. A hired killer, *sicario*, could be bought for a mere $10 US. Killings were by no means all drug related. Getting rid of someone offered a simple solution to family feuds and business deals gone awry. Colombians had grown used to murder. There was no "dark undercurrent" in Colombia as I read about in detective novels. Not at all. It was right on the surface, one wave of evil after another.

"But come inside," she beckoned, her deep-set eyes eager. I was glad to get inside. I was sick and tired of violence and had no interest to see a dead body.

In her front room a flowered cloth covered a cot that served as a couch by day and her son's bed at night. Red geraniums in metal coffee tins happily shouldered each other across the high windowsill. An odd odour filled the room. I sniffed. What was it? It was a smell I didn't know, a smell I was finding repugnant. I wondered if Harold felt the same but there was no chance to get into his line of sight with my raised eyebrow.

"Would you like to see the house?" she asked in the traditional Colombian manner. And away we went. Two small rooms made up the ground floor. At the back, plain wooden stairs led up to the second floor. The peculiar smell got stronger and stronger as we climbed.

Upstairs was a bedroom that doubled as dining room. A bed stood by one wall and against the other wall was a simple wooden table and benches. Next to the table a striped curtain hid the bathroom.

She led us into the kitchen, a narrow room with a brightly curtained window.

"Do you smell the *mazamorra*? See!" She lifted the lid on an enormous aluminum pot on the gas burner. The distinct smell poured from the open lid.

"I made enough for the whole week. Maybe it's ready now and you can enjoy some. How wonderful you came exactly today!"

Harold and I shot each other worried glances.

"Oh, thank you," I smiled. "But we're not hungry. We just finished our lunch."

"Have you had *mazamorra* before?"

We shook our heads.

"You've never had it before? Impossible!"

She laughed. The Colombians of the barrios were always puzzled about how we'd spent our pre-Colombian lives. We seemed to be ignorant of the most basic elements of life.

Alicia, still laughing, chose a cup into which she poured a small sample of the hot liquid. To this she added a good pour of cold milk. Then she handed us the cup and two spoons.

Harold and I stood huddled over the cup, lifting the spoons slowly to our lips. Kernels of tough-skinned, non-sweet corn swam in a white pond of thin cornstarch. No salt or sugar, but only the one odorous spice that was making my knees weak. That was silly. I should be a much stronger missionary, otherwise, why come thousands of miles from home?

Alicia watched in eager silence as we finished. Feeling triumphant we put down the empty cup. We had done our duty.

"How do you like it?" she asked.

Harold nodded and forced a weak smile.

"Very good," I lied.

"So, you like it! I'll give you a proper serving."

She reached up to a shelf, whipped down two large bowls and into each one poured a huge ladle of the brew. In went dollops of cold milk.

I threw a desperate look at Harold. He had folded his arms and looked resigned to his fate. Only a brief bitter glance said, "Look what comes of carelessly tossing out lies."

Alicia carried the bowls to the other room and set them on the table, gesturing for us to sit down across from each other. Then she pulled a stool to the end of the table and sat down.

Oh Lord, she intends to watch us take each mouthful.

Harold, the good sport, dug in. Slowly, I stirred the corn kernels around the edges and then looked up at Alicia with a smile. But after three stirs and three smiles, no new idea came to me.

Then, blessedly, the doorbell rang. God answering prayer.

"Permiso, excuse me," Alicia stood up and started down the stairs.

I leaped from my chair.

I have been accused at various times of being uncoordinated but anyone witnessing my actions that day would have admired my agility.

Clutching the bowl, I turned to the bathroom curtain behind me. In one smooth move, I raised the curtain, poured the soup into the toilet bowl, flushed the toilet and spun around, back to my bench.

And none too soon.

I heard steps on the staircase. I was in my seat holding the spoon over my bowl as Alicia approached. Harold shook his head at me, but I saw he still had half a bowl to go. And I was all done!

There was only one problem.

From behind the striped curtain came noises. Hiss! Hiss! Sputter. The toilet tank was protesting.

Hiss! Hiss! Sputter. It wouldn't stop.

Alicia, back in her spot, raised her eyebrows at my empty bowl. "Would you like a little more?"

"No," I was calm and careful this time. "I'm quite full now, *gracias*." Harold dutifully kept spooning in his soup to the last drop.

Later as we bounced along home in the jeep, Harold broke the silence.

"She knew."

"She did not know," I stated firmly.

"You couldn't use the bathroom and swallow a bowl of the stuff at the same time. And she was only gone a few minutes. She knew."

I sighed. Pride in my quick-witted solution was starting to fade. I had tossed out someone else's precious food. Great missionaries, spiritual giants, are able to swallow live worms, crunch on insects and eat monkey's head stew.

I was a dwarf, not one of the giants.

22   What's the Spanish for nails?

The building where we met for church was the only Mennonite Brethren Church in Medellín. "Oh, this is not really a church at all!" we had said when we first saw it.

It was a basement built into a hillside, an eyesore that had waited years for an actual sanctuary to be built on it.

We thought that if the church sanctuary could be completed at the street level, it would give our people something to be proud of. And besides, we needed a bigger space. On Sundays now, the basement space was crowded. Benches were carried in from the adjoining Sunday School rooms for the new people attending. And for the Sunday School time, I had even had one of the young men install a tarp over a corner on the open concrete pad above because we needed another classroom.

Harold and I lobbied the mission board for funds. We wrote to all our friends, family and acquaintances asking them to contribute. Soon money started pouring in.

Harold began to plan. He had yet to learn the Spanish name for nails and screws, but he fearlessly forged ahead. His experience was building Canadian homes with wood and drywall. But construction in Colombia was done with cement, steel and adobe bricks. A learning experience.

There was no money to hire a contractor. Harold went ahead and, step by step, took charge. By June 1988, ten months into our first term in Colombia, Harold had launched into the construction work, climbing a steep learning curve—new rules, new materials and new methods.

At the same time the regular church work continued. There was a baptism in June, a church retreat to plan for and a prayer vigil. There were new converts to plan Bible studies for and, to top it all, a strange young man had shown up at our church threatening to hold street meetings about healing outside the home of a member who was gravely ill.

"He's a royal pain!" I declared in our missionary team meeting.

The others agreed. "He preaches that all illness is a punishment from God for having too little faith. And he's persuading some of our youth—"

"Oh yeah, when I prayed in church, 'Your will be done,' he accused me of having too little faith. Anyway, I called that home this morning to comfort the family and warn them that if he shows up, they mustn't think we sent him!"

When Albert Enns, our senior team member, realized that Harold meant to forge ahead and build the church sanctuary he offered to help. He drafted designs and came up with the plan to have a double-arched doorway and arched windows, adding beauty as well as functionality.

That first summer in Colombia, June - August 1988, was packed with activity. We hosted a work team from Canada who came to help construct the church sanctuary. Linda and Galen hosted the girls and we hosted the guys. I switched from packing kids' lunch kits to filling brown bags with hearty meals for Harold and the young men.

The main pillars of the sanctuary needed to be heavily reinforced with steel bars for earthquake protection. Then, the Canadian girls and guys mixed concrete for the pillars using shovels and wheelbarrows. Matthew enjoyed the company of the young men and went with them each day to work on the project.

Between supervising the work, Harold made trips all over the city with our jeep buying supplies and tools. He came home each day exhausted. One of his biggest challenges was coordinating Colombian workers with the non-Spanish speaking volunteers from Canada.

"These Canadian boys are pushing to work faster, faster. But it's the Colombians who understand better how things are done here. Always this tension."

In spite of differences, the Canadians infused us and the church with new energy and optimism. And we needed that.

After a few weeks of work the Canadians returned home. Construction continued with one or two Colombian fellows from the church working full time with Harold.

I was up at six those mornings, packing construction crew lunches for Harold, Matthew and the two young Colombians. But, too often, I'd step into the kitchen, push the light switch, and—nothing. No electricity.

Harold and young men mix concrete.

Matthew helps his dad at the construction site.

"Do you have electricity in *your* house?" I asked a neighbour. They motioned with their hands—off and on.

"Well," I grumbled, "electricity has been out in half our house for seven straight days now. And it's the half of the house that includes the kitchen!"

Stress was mounting, one incident after another. As Harold was crossing the street near the church, a motorcycle ran into him and badly bruised his leg.

Then a few hours later his jeep hit another car, just denting our fender and fortunately not denting the other.

It wasn't the best day to come home and find the house still without electricity, me battling bronchitis and hoping my dear husband would dash out again to get more medicine. A perfectly awful day.

It was time for a break. Maybe we could squeeze in a summer holiday.

 ## 23   Getting away from it all

June 1, 1988 had been the first day of summer vacation from school for our kids. It was also an historic day in Colombia.

Three months earlier, in March, the mayors, *alcaldes*, of more than 1000 municipalities had been elected by popular vote for the first time in Colombian history. Previously, the governors of each province had appointed the mayors. Wednesday, June 1, was the day on which the newly elected mayors took office.

The country held its breath expecting that the change would spark violence. The government banned all ceremonies, so no celebrations were planned anywhere.

On this first day of vacation I could have slept in but I had a violent dream and woke at 6 a.m. I pulled on my purple gingham housecoat, slipped downstairs and made a cup of peppermint tea. Then I shut myself into the office with a picture book of Manitoba landscapes. It was comforting to see wide fields of grain where it was safe to wander. The grand sunsets. Open roads and meadows without threat of being accosted or gunned down.

Ironically, at 7 a.m. just as I was settling my nerves there was a gunshot somewhere on our block. No one rushed from their home to see what it was. Everyone heard, feared and from behind their barred doors and windows wondered what happened now. I contented myself with knowing that our kids were happy. They seemed at peace even though they needed to stay indoors on this day, which was unpredictable.

I had planned projects for the kids during the summer break to keep them occupied and to teach them skills they didn't learn in the classroom: cooking, sewing on buttons, flower arranging. So, after breakfast I laid cloth and stuffing over the dining room table and got Matt and Becky started on their first project—tying new quilts for the young boys' bunkbeds. The cloth sported a happy collection of boats, trains and airplanes in bright yellow, red and blue. I marked a pattern of dots across the fabric and they tied the knots.

Becky ties colourful quilts for the bunk beds.

That evening Harold and I left the children at home to attend a prayer meeting and Bible study at Mabel's house, just a block or so from the church. We parked our jeep on the street right in front of the house and walked up a flight of stairs. Her home was on the second floor with a balcony that faced the street. Mabel indicated that Harold and I should sit right in the balcony doorway where a refreshing breeze ruffled the curtains. About a dozen adults from the church sat around the room and a young leader started the meeting. Through the open window came all the sounds of an evening in the barrio. Radios pumping out salsa or merengue. Teenagers talking and laughing.

Suddenly a fierce BANG! sounded in the street and a bright light lit up the night sky. Everyone wondered aloud, "What was that?" One of the young men ran downstairs and soon came back to report.

"Someone exploded a small bomb outside the house. Just a few metres from your jeep."

"No one got hurt?"

"I couldn't see anyone hurt or any damage, just a burning thing on the ground. Your jeep looks okay."

Mabel stood up and approached us. "*Hermanos*, please, move away from the window. Come sit here on the far side of the room."

We moved. I felt uneasy. The prayer time continued.

But it was different now.

In the Colombians' prayers they made special mention of our family, noting that as foreigners we were in greater danger and would God please give us protection.

For the first time since coming to Colombia I felt a specific fear come over me, a suffocating fear. All the way home in the jeep I prayed for God's wing to cover us and lift my fear.

Back at home the house was quiet, the children in their beds. I slept well that night and woke optimistic.

I sat down to write to my parents, assuring them they should not be worried for their grandkids' safety. I knew they also worried about the children's development while in Colombia so I sent them a little summary of the upsides.

"Andrew learned to read this year and spends hours paging through books or reading to Conrad. He broke his arm playing at school and we didn't even know it until finally a day later, we took him for X-rays. The brave little guy had just kept putting up with the pain! Becky got a leash for Mitzi and now we let her walk the dog twice a day together with the two little boys. They go up and down on our street basically back and forth in front of the house.

Andy reads for Conrad and Mitzi.

"Conrad at four and a half has really matured. He has good table manners, is very neat. Each of his four years has been in a different country so he hasn't felt as secure as the others. More security and a stable place have done wonders. For him this is home and Canada will be a foreign land. The other three at least look forward to returning for a furlough.

"I'm making Becky a new dress, big checks in blue and pink. She is so excited she hovers over the sewing machine to watch me. She's learning to sew, too.

"Matthew plays piano all day if we let him. It's good to have the old classics ring through the house: Beethoven, Mozart, Chopin. He gets along well with his piano teacher and is reading a lot. His current book is Packer's *Knowing God*. He received the sportsmanship award chosen by the students and says this has been the best year of his life. We thank God for the new teachers, the McMonagles, who have been such a positive influence."

The second day of vacation was busy with a lot of phone counselling, Harold and I taking turns talking with distressed church members. But in the evening after the youngest two were in bed, we sat on the living room sofa talking about how we might have a family summer vacation.

"With a work team staying with us this summer," I said, "there's no family time at home. The kids have worked hard this year, getting really good grades. It would be nice to relax together away from the house."

Then, the McMonagles, who lived on the school compound, called to say they would be away for several days and invited us to stay in their home.

"Yayyy! We can play outside all day!" Andy told Conrad and the two jumped with glee.

"I'm going to teach these kids to make a campfire," Harold said. We borrowed a tent and aimed to give the kids a Canadian camping experience. We packed our jeep with wieners and buns and trundled off across the city toward Bello.

Inside the compound there were three or four houses quite a distance apart, not in sight of each other and separated by graceful stands of tall bamboo, banana trees and rows of coffee plants. McMonagles' house was a welcoming cottage with airy rooms, tasteful decor and the treasure of full bookshelves.

Harold set up the tent behind the house. It was a small pup tent with room for only two. The first night we planned that ten-year-old Becky and Andy, six, would sleep in the tent. They were excited at the prospect.

Harold and I wished we could recreate for the kids the kind of summers we had in Canada when we worked in a northern wilderness camp on Simonhouse Lake in Manitoba. There, the cry of the loons lulled us to sleep at night. In the morning we woke to the sound of wild deer munching grass outside our cabin window. Harold had led several canoe trips through a maze of lakes, their water so pure we just scooped and drank.

It was pitch dark by seven o'clock and I began to doubt the wisdom of leaving the kids out in the yard.

"Harold, remember that the guerrillas invaded this compound just a few years ago? I'm a bit nervous to—"

"It's fine. We're right close by. Nothing can happen."

"I don't think I'll be able to sleep if they're out there."

After a few more back and forths, Harold relented, "Okay. Once they're asleep, I'll carry Becky inside and I'll sleep out there with Andy."

Then we heard a loud BANG!

"That's a rifle shot," Harold said.

"It sounds very close. Maybe at the upper *finca*. I sure hope it's not up at the Brubachers' house."

Over the next hour and a half we heard eight more shots.

"That's too much. We've got to get the kids in."

Harold carried in both sleeping kids and we all slept indoors. At night it started to rain, so in the morning we told the kids it had been too wet to sleep outside. We often tried to avoid talk of violence. Our aim was to allow them to enjoy life without anxiety.

Then, at 5 p.m. that day a bomb went off close enough to rattle the windows.

"So much for getting away from it all," I said.

It didn't faze Harold. He sent all the kids out to scour the grounds for firewood. They came back with armfuls of branches and twigs. How excited they were to build a fire and have a wiener roast!

Harold rallies the troops.

Back home after our few days away, our schedule got hectic again. Harold went weeks with no day off, coordinating the construction work at the church and continuing the pastoral work. Sunday for us was always a major workday, teaching classes, conducting church services morning and evening, making appointments for those who asked for a visit.

Harold's body reacted with a severe sinus infection that did not clear up. So, after hosting yet another work crew in our home that summer Harold announced in mid-August, "Let's go to Cartagena— to the ocean!"

"How? Fly?"

"No way. We'll drive. It's not that far. One day."

"But we have no map and—"

"It's basically north. Few main roads. Probably find our way easily. It'll be perfect."

The kids were thrilled with the prospect of driving to the ocean, so plans were made. We left at 5 a.m., the jeep loaded with beach clothes, cheese sandwiches, dried guava squares, a dozen small bags of Fritos and a big thermos of ice water.

I love maps and I love road trips. But with no map I was uneasy of what might lie ahead and how we'd know which roads to take. But Harold was so confident, I tried to catch his spirit of adventure.

A few hours out of Medellín traffic slowed and up ahead we saw a long line of trucks, jeeps and buses that wound snakelike along a narrow highway cut into the mountainside. Traffic came to a full stop and we waited. We noticed the Colombians getting out of their vehicles and consulting with each other.

"Wonder what's up," Harold muttered. "Doesn't look anything like a military or guerrilla stop. Maybe an accident? Your Spanish is good. Find out what's up."

I got out of the jeep and walked toward a sturdy woman in overalls returning from further up the line.

"Qué pasó aqui?" I asked her. What's happened?

Her mouth opened and out came a fierce stream of Spanish words I tried to capture.

I nodded. *"Ah, sí."*

Her hands flew from side to side in wild gestures.

I murmured. *"Ah, ja."* After a few minutes of this I said, *"Gracias"* and climbed back into the jeep.

"What? What's happened?" Everyone shouted at once. I turned to look at the kids in the back seats and shook my head.

"Sorry. I've no idea what she said."

"But you were nodding your head the whole time!"

"Well, I did catch something about 'a few hours.' So, we're probably stuck here for a while."

Groans.

It turned out there had been a landslide. No one could come or go. But it was an adventure and we were up for adventure. We made a game of eating our picnic lunch in the jeep and, after three hours, one lane was cleared and we limped forward.

It took fourteen hours to travel from Medellín to Cartagena. Once there, all six of us crowded into one hotel room and sank gratefully into sleep. The next day we enjoyed jumping waves in the warm, foamy salt water. We made plans to visit the historic sites and Harold arranged to do some long-awaited sailing.

After supper on our first full day we returned to the beach.

Sundown was the loveliest time of day, yet no one was on the beach. It was completely deserted. We couldn't understand why. Tourists were seated in the bars and cafés alongside the ocean but not on the beach. The tide was coming in, the waves lovely and plump, barrelling onto the sands. Harold and the children went to jump in the waves while I stayed on the beach guarding our shoes and watches. Shouts of glee came from the kids as Harold took turns picking them up and tossing them into oncoming waves.

Suddenly a café owner came running down the beach toward me.

"*Señora! Tiburones!* They come at this time of day. You should know that if your husband calls for help, no one will go out to rescue him."

I thanked him and settled back on my towel. *Tiburones?* That was a word I didn't know. Likely means the fast eddies swirling around the rocks. But that man doesn't know my husband. Harold's not going to get out of the water just because someone else thinks there's a risk. He *lives* for risk!

When Harold finally tired and waded toward me, I mentioned that the man had warned of *tiburones.*

"*Tiburones!* Sharks!" He spun around and we both dashed toward the water waving our arms and yelling at the kids. What a relief when they were back on dry land. So much for my superior Spanish!

After a glorious week in Cartagena without obligations, without houseguests and building crews, without sticky church issues to sort out, we piled again into the jeep for the ride home.

Seeing roadside stands loaded with fruit, Harold stopped the jeep and went fruit crazy. During his childhood and youth, fresh fruit had been extremely rare. For him, it was gold. He bought a dozen huge mangos, some guanabanas, two bags of guavas and a whole tree branch— about three feet long— full of mini bananas.

Harold finds a gold mine.

I rolled my eyes. "Who's going to eat all this?"

The kids obligingly slid close together on the two side benches in the back of the jeep so that the banana branch could hang suspended inside the rear door.

Down the road, the fruit came in handy. The landslide that had delayed us eight days earlier had re-occurred. We were stuck in our jeep, not moving for three hours while rain poured in buckets outside. We were nose to tail with an open cattle truck. To pass the time we made a game of getting the kids to guess which cow would next raise its head to moo. A right guess earned a small treat and helped to pass the time.

Then another scenario took shape.

Next to us on the shoulder of the road, an elderly farmer and his daughter set up four rough wooden poles. They strung a plastic sheet over the poles. One corner of this makeshift roof they slanted downward. There they set an open pot to catch the rain streaming off the tarp. Under the shelter of the tarp they set up a charcoal burner, poured the collected rainwater into a pot of coffee grounds and *Presto*—a coffee shop!

Soon stranded drivers and passengers were lining up to pay for a much-appreciated cup of hot *tinto*. Colombians are endlessly resourceful.

 ## 24   Up in the Andes

When we returned to Medellín, it was time for the whole church to take a break. Since starting to work with the church people, Harold and I had often asked ourselves, "How can we boost the spirits of our church people?" Morale was so low. They struggled day after day with the pain of poverty, the sense of powerlessness and the prospect of little future change.

"A camp weekend outside the city would help," Harold suggested.

I agreed. "That always brings people together. Builds unity." In Canada at summer camps we had seen firsthand the positive impact of the outdoors on city people.

The church elders agreed that a *campamento* was a great idea.

"But," they said, "the people are poor. No one can pay for such an outing." Together with the elders we made two plans to solve the problem.

One—the families could begin months ahead of time to bring a small contribution to the church treasurer each week and in this way pay for transportation, food and the camp fees in installment payments. The church people were very happy with that plan.

Two—I suggested the women put on a sidewalk sale, a bazaar as they called it, and offer food and used clothing. They jumped at the idea.

The bazaar was set for a Saturday. It was the first time the church ladies had ever held one so they asked me to organize it. To my Canadian brain, a reasonable time for a sidewalk sale to begin was 2 p.m. Then it would likely close around 4 p.m. in time to go home and make supper.

I told Luis, the holder of the church key, "I'll come to church at 12:30 on Saturday to organize tables and get ready."

"I'll come at that time, too," said Delia, the woman working with me on planning.

That Saturday it poured. We arrived at church at 12:45 to find the outer gate locked. Conrad and Becky were with me to help out and the three of us huddled under umbrellas while Harold drove to retrieve a key and to ask Delia what was happening.

"Delia is busy making *natilla* to sell," he reported when he came back. "Another woman, Helena, is there in Delia's kitchen grinding meat to make stuffed potatoes."

"I guess we're on our own for set-up," I said. Since it was raining, we organized the benches and tables indoors. My North American brain told me that we advertised the starting time as 2 p.m. and we had to be ready then. I had lots to learn.

By 2:30 very few people had shown up. Rain kept coming down in sheets. Finally, at 3:30 the rain cleared and we carried everything upstairs to the sidewalk. So, by 4 p.m., the time I thought it would end, the sidewalk sale actually got started. By 5:30 most of the food was sold. I thought the church women would call it quits but they wanted to go on with the bazaar until dusk. And I was surprised at how much fun I was having. My Spanish had reached the point where I could catch on to most jokes they told, even in rapid speech, so I thoroughly enjoyed all the interactions.

Neighbours lined up at the church yard sale.

We finally closed down at 7 p.m. There was some *mazamorra* left and *arroz con leche* that the women decided to sell the next morning after the church service. It was a great surprise to everyone that we cleared 16,000 pesos, about $80.00 Canadian.

"Quite something for this little group," I told Harold. "And great for team spirit!"

When the weekend arrived for the church *campamento*, spirits were high. A hired bus took everyone up the mountain to 8000 feet. At that altitude the weather was cold for Medellín folk who enjoy the same warm temperature all year round. But in spite of the cold, the people were thrilled.

"It's so relaxing to be in the country!" Elsa exclaimed. "I see trees instead of buildings. I hear birds instead of buses."

There were a few low adobe buildings built in the economical style, which meant the mortar oozed out between the bricks making the walls rough both on the outside and the inside of the buildings. Women and men slept in separate sections with separate bathrooms.

I slept on the bottom of a triple bunk bed. Becky climbed into the one above me. We couldn't sit upright in the bunks and that made me think of Corrie ten Boom's description of the concentration camp where there was only about two feet of space between each bunk. But we were fortunate that our only enemy was the cold.

It was very cold at night, high in the Andes. I hadn't packed enough blankets and hoped my old nemesis, bronchitis, would not show up. I shivered all night long and then woke to the prospect of a cold shower.

Harold and I were in charge of the weekend but had never before experienced a Colombian camp outing. Who knew you had to have a way to purify all drinking water? Or that someone had to be assigned to get up at five each morning to help the cooks grind corn for breakfast arepas? Or that all Colombians get up *before* the wake-up bell and make more noise than a dozen buses and every single one right down to the youngest takes a cold shower every day?

Somehow, we got clean water to drink and everyone got fed. At mealtime the cooks handed each person a plastic bowl of food: rice and beans or rice and a sauce. They handed each person a plastic cup of *aguapanela*, hardened sugar cane dissolved in water. We sat on benches at bare wood tables. After everyone was through the line, the pass-thru window was put down and that was it. There were no seconds and no desserts, but no one expected any, so everyone left the table content.

I was delighted to see our kids fit in well, playing the games with the other kids and eating and drinking whatever was served. Never a question or complaint. What a relief. Harold and I had made the choice to work in Colombia and we had hoped our kids would adapt. It was gratifying to see it happen.

Saturday afternoon everyone was out on a grassy field participating in group games. Suddenly BANG! BANG! Shots rang out from the other side of the fence. Edgar, in his sixties the oldest church member, threw himself flat on the ground, his face down and arms out, with no thought of the nice clothes he was wearing. No one else reacted that way.

We didn't know what the shots were about but at least, it was determined, they had not been directed at our gathering. Edgar jumped up then, dusted off his clothes and looked sheepish. He had lived through *La Violencia*. When I saw how strong the fear was that had instantly gripped him, it told me a lot about how much people had suffered in Colombia. I felt sad for him. He was such a kind, generous person and he looked embarrassed to have shown his fear so nakedly.

"We're going to build a *fogata*!" the fellows announced on Saturday night.

"What's a *fogata*?"

"The biggest bonfire you've ever seen!"

It was built by placing logs in a square, leaving a space in the centre. A very long bamboo pole was then inserted in the centre, pointing straight up to the sky. Everyone gathered around. As the fire got hotter, the air inside the lowest section of bamboo expanded and burst open with a big loud POP. Everyone jumped with delight, laughing and clapping. Each successive section of bamboo heated and burst as the evening went on.

We all stayed up late, singing around the fire. The Colombians freely showed their emotions, often hugging each other. Some people, new to the church, found themselves in tears.

I shed a few tears of joy myself.

25   The doorbell rang

A few weeks later, Monday morning, was our kids' first day back to school. Harold drove them after taking Conrad to a neighbourhood pre-school. We had company coming at suppertime, but till then, I had the house to myself.

Chapter 25

"This, my dear," I told the mirror, "will be a glorious day! I'll read for an hour, have an extra coffee, dress leisurely—"

The doorbell rang.

Who drops in at 7:45 Monday morning? It was Guillermo from church, a university student.

Why, Lord? Why?

I was in my housecoat and very un-made-up but I felt I had to invite him in. The extra coffee I'd planned, I shared with him, and toast as well. I fell into my missionary mode and put leisure lady out of mind.

We had a fine talk. Guillermo put some of his life questions to me and I challenged him about his priorities, about how to spend his time more wisely. He seemed to appreciate my perspective and thanked me before leaving for his studies.

Well, could I still salvage some free time?

But soon Harold returned, and shortly after that, a car pulled up at our driveway. No one in our church group owned a car. It was Emiliano, one of our church men who worked as a chauffeur.

"I have an hour free and was nearby," he exclaimed. "Such good fortune!"

I served him and Harold a *café con leche*. When the hour was up, he stood at the door and turned back with a question.

"I just started this new job and I want my boss's car as shiny as I can make it. May I wash the car on your driveway later on? Just this once. I won't make a habit of it."

That afternoon he reappeared and began washing the car. He spent one and a half hours scrubbing and polishing. Stalling, I thought. Harold had mentioned that a pastor and his wife from Bogotá were coming for supper. So, naturally, since Emiliano was there when company showed up, he had a plate of food together with the rest of us. Who knows, maybe his own food supply had run short.

That evening Harold and I kept the Bogotá couple talking for quite some time. He was an experienced and dedicated pastor with a lovely wife. We were fascinated to hear their slant on how the churches in different regions of the country were doing and how they viewed the influence of former missionaries, a touchy topic.

I stayed up an extra hour that evening reading on the living room sofa. I had missed the glorious morning I'd longed for and tomorrow would start early with the 8 a.m. missionary team meeting. After that, Harold and I had an afternoon appointment to deal with a church member accused of unfaithfulness to her husband.

I settled on the sofa with my book. A brief escape into a whodunit would be just the thing.

But no.

"Harold, come look!" I called. A huge black moth with a wingspan of eight inches clung to the side of our bookcase.

"Oh," he exclaimed coming down the stairs, "it's beautiful! That's a moth? Look at the markings—"

"Please take it out."

What I didn't know then was that Colombia is the second-most diverse country in the world for its variety of creatures. The moth was indeed an exceptional visitor.

"Please take him out," I begged. "I've had enough today of unplanned visitors. If the Queen herself shows up at the door, I'll say, 'Wrong castle!'"

26 Caught in a tug-of-war

I grew up in the fishbowl of a pastor's family life, the third of seven kids. We were to be the model of good behaviour for the church and the community. And our home, the parsonage, was not our castle, not the place in which to relax and be ourselves. Instead it formed the base of operations to meet the needs of others. I was trained to show a cheerful face in every situation. If I had complaints, only my journal heard them.

I felt disoriented in Medellín. Something was missing. A simple enjoyment in Canada for relieving stress was taking a drive in the car. Here though, a drive with the unexpected police checkpoints caused rather than relieved stress. I confessed my frustration to my journal.

"Today I just want everything to be normal again. Normal—as in Canadian. I want to get behind the wheel of our station wagon in small-town Manitoba, drive the five minutes to our grocery store. I want to be back there where I was healthy. I want soft rugs, not cement floors, and I want to watch an English TV show and to pass someone on the street and say Hello instead of *Buenos días*."

The needs of the church and its people were never-ending. Often, we felt as if we had been dropped into a desert with one litre of water and faced an entire camp of dehydrated nomads, an endless sea of need. Our job of calibrating the urgency of the need added its own stress.

Without our usual outlets from tension—Harold's sports interests, my writing life, our friends—we started to have more disagreements.

"Harold, you had a long day today. Your entire morning in that mission meeting. Then just a quick lunch, then a meeting with the church elders for two hours, then you led the Wednesday evening service at church. That's more than a full day's work. And it goes on and on every day. Plus, weekends. Why can't missionaries work an eight-hour day like everyone else?"

"Missionaries should do the work the Lord tells them to do, not what the wife tells them."

"Well, maybe sometimes the wife and the Lord might have similar ideas."

Silence.

It's true that missionary work thrived on our sense of duty. Living on donated money, supported by others, we felt we didn't deserve time away from mission work.

Once, I saw a Saturday afternoon puppet show, *Sleeping Beauty*, advertised in the newspaper. We bought tickets. It would be the first outing of this kind for our kids since coming to Medellín. But when Saturday came and it was time to go, Harold balked.

"Is this what I came to Medellín for, to take kids to a puppet show?"

I understood.

We still went, but it was hard, because we knew of several Colombians waiting for a visit from us, to say nothing of the lessons and sermon to prepare for the next day. Though Harold loved to play with the children and sometimes took them kite flying on Nutibara Hill, he and I both felt the constant tug-of-war between mission work and raising our four children.

Harold and Becky fly a kite at the top of Nutibara Hill.

For two years before arriving in Medellín, we were both immersed in studies in California, then in Costa Rica. In Medellín I felt I finally had more time to be a mom again. The kids seemed to appreciate that I was at home more now. They'd become more relaxed and more obedient. I enjoyed having time to talk with them.

One evening when I was recovering from bronchitis and all the kids had caught colds, too, I checked on Becky and found her reading before falling asleep with Mitzi beside her.

I went into the little boys' bedroom and spread Vaporub on Andy's chest to relieve his cough. I rubbed Conrad's back to help him fall asleep, and I sang to him. When I sang "Jesus Loves Me," he loved it. To him it was novel to hear that children's song, not old hat like it was to me.

"Can't you wub my back evwee night?" Conrad asked.

Oh, if only I could have that time back again. What a tug-of-war it was. Give my time to family or give it to the church? Many nights I was away at meetings or I rushed the kids off to bed in order to sit down to plan a lesson or a talk for the next day.

In Matthew's room I found him engrossed over a checkerboard. "Look, Mom, I invented this new game. It's a lot like chess but has more action."

"That is so neat!" Then it struck me that he likely wished his father was free more evenings. Harold liked to play chess with him but was kept busy with the many facets of the church work.

The church construction had turned out to be more challenging than expected. A tall stack of receipts on Harold's desk showed the dozens of purchases he'd made. There were no hardware stores as we knew them. Nails were sold at the nail store. Tools were sold at a tool store. Bricks in the brick store. He put many miles on our jeep gathering supplies.

Finally, on a Monday in October we enjoyed a reprieve—Canadian Thanksgiving Day.

With whom should we celebrate?

Our fellow Canadians! Our kids' favorite teachers, Ruth and Trevor McMonagle and their children, Natalie and Graham.

But what will we serve?

Ruth and I put our heads together.

There were no turkeys in Medellín so we roasted chicken with homemade stuffing. No cranberries, so we cooked up applesauce. Also, carrots au gratin, potatoes, gravy and pickles. There were no pumpkins but we made do with a squash pie.

Thanksgiving at our table: Dorothy, Matthew, Rebecca, Natalie, Trevor, Ruth, Graham, Andy, Conrad.

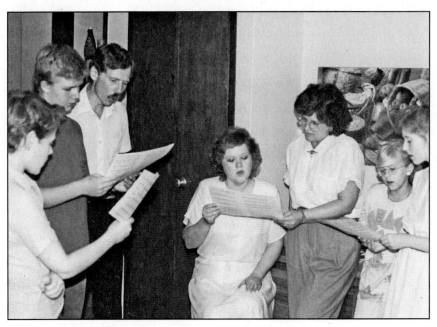

We tried 4-part harmonies.

We felt extremely wealthy in food and friendship! Gathered around our table we relaxed and laughed together.

They liked music just as we did and Ruth suggested, "Why don't we sing those English songs we haven't heard for a while?"

So, the children, rather than running off to play, stayed at table and we two families sang one song after another in English. Then we graduated to sheet music and had fun doing four-part harmonies.

It was glorious, a truly Canadian Thanksgiving. Our hearts felt full.

27   And this, too

Faith in God was the bedrock on which I had built my life since childhood. God was personal to me. I repeatedly turned to the Bible for guidance and comfort. My daily readings and prayer were not mere piety. I longed to be in close touch with God and tried to understand what he had in mind for me. I never doubted that his Spirit guided me directly.

I heard the cry of my own heart when I read in the Bible Moses' cry in the desert, "Why have you given me the responsibility for all these people?"

God's answer to Moses comforted me, "Is there any limit to my power?"

One morning I read how Moses in a time of indecision told others, "Wait until I receive instructions from the Lord." I discussed that with Harold.

"Maybe we rush into too many ministry jobs here like counseling those we think need it. Maybe we should wait more for the Lord's signal to go ahead." We agreed to move more slowly but then we felt pressed when the people asked us for help.

One day we visited a woman about ten years older than me. "Will you please pray and fast with me?" she asked us. "I have so many problems. I'm very afraid."

We fasted for twenty-four hours then went back to see her.

"Scary things are happening in my house—I saw a vision of a man who I know is in the occult. I saw him threaten me, put needles at my throat. What can I do? I'm so afraid."

We felt out of our depth but we explained that God's power, the power of the good, is much stronger than the power of evil. We prayed special prayers for her and gave her printed prayers she could say whenever the fear came over her.

The next day she called to say she had slept much better. We felt relieved. But we also wondered whether ours had been a band-aid solution when more was required. We started a search for answers in books and from other missionaries' experiences.

The next day's activity was a change from home visitations. Harold drove Benji's family to the cemetery to see his grave. They hadn't been back since the funeral because it was so far for them to go and the bus was expensive for such a large group. Silvia and all her eight children squeezed into our jeep, no problem!

After visiting the gravesite, Harold brought them to our house for afternoon coffee. By now I had learned the Colombian way and I served each one their own plate with a ham sandwich, oatmeal cookies, juice and *café con leche*. I was happy to have them over; they were a respectful, interested-in-everything sort of family.

Family at graveside.

The next week's dinner guests were not as cheerful. It was an elderly couple. The talk turned to the shaky political situation.

"In our country there is a total decay of morality. No justice. Have you heard—people say the police are now in the habit of killing the young people they arrest. If it's on drug charges or robbery, doesn't matter."

"A very sad state of affairs," agreed the wife. "As soon as anyone speaks out against something bad, more likely than not they get shot soon after."

"Oh, yes, like those brave journalists. How many have been killed now and for—"

"At least eighty journalists in the past ten years. I read that just this week."

After we kissed the couple goodbye in the traditional way, I sat on the sofa musing.

I suddenly wished to be elsewhere.

Anywhere.

"It's hours of solitude I'm craving," I told Harold. "Hours of quiet reflecting. I wish I could write and evaluate all the stuff happening around us."

"No time—"

"So why did God make me this way—to want to write and reflect—and then call me to work in this challenging country? And bless me with four kids?"

"And," added Harold, "with a husband who keeps you busy."

I rolled my eyes.

Harold shrugged and, trying to lighten my mood, quoted Scripture out of context, "The Lord's ways are past finding out."

My spirit wasn't settled as each day brought a new challenge on which to focus my attention.

At a Wednesday night prayer meeting that week, Freddy asked, "Please pray for my family. We are fifteen people in my house and this week my cousin was arrested for drug dealing and—"

"How old is he?"

"Thirteen. If my father finds out he'll make our whole family move. It's not safe there. And another thing, my sister is crying because no one knows if they'll ever see my cousin again. Maybe they'll just torture him and shoot him—that's what's happened to others around here."

We prayed for him, but I wondered, *Am I really here? This is a crazy time. Is it really all happening?*

28   Gonna put on my long white robe

Our first baptism! This was an exciting moment for us as a new pastor couple since Harold had not baptized anyone before. It was exciting, too, for the ones being baptized. New members who wished to join the church were required to be baptized by immersion, getting submerged in water. That was the requirement at the time for membership in a Mennonite Brethren church. Baptismal candidates must reach the 'age of consent' and must understand the meaning of the act.

Our church building had no baptismal tank but the Baptist church in the neighbouring barrio of La Milagrosa kindly lent us their sanctuary. It was easy for the people to get to, within walking distance of our church.

This was the same church building in which we held Benji's funeral service. In fact, he had hoped to be baptized. Instead, two brothers of his, moved by Benji's faith that gave him and his mother such optimism in his final days, now took his spot among the baptismal candidates.

The ceremony would take place while Harold stood waist deep in water, so he'd have no printed notes to follow. He needed to memorize the series of questions put to each candidate as well as the formal declaration proclaimed before dunking them.

Everything in Spanish, of course.

I had a wifely anxiety about this as Harold was not at his best where memorization was required. He enjoyed more spontaneous interactions. Would he get through it in a suitably sacred and formal way or would he "pull a Harold" which we knew meant anything could happen.

I held my breath as he stepped down into the baptismal tank and in turn, as each candidate joined him, I could feel the congregation holding their breath, too. But Harold asked all the right questions and ended with the formal declaration, "On the confession of your faith I now baptize you in the name of the Father, the Son and the Holy Spirit. Amen."

Then, *swoosh* and *swoosh*. And the church burst into song as each member surfaced.

I felt tears as Benji's brothers proclaimed their "I wills." I heard others reaching for tissues, too. Afterwards, we shared cake and coffee in the midst of many hugs and congratulations.

Baptism in the tank of the Baptist Church in La Milagrosa.

A few months later, four more people who had taken the membership classes asked to be baptized. Elizabeth Tieszen, senior missionary, came up from Cali to help celebrate and to see how we were succeeding as new missionaries.

"Let's just hope everything goes off without a hitch," I said to Harold.

However, as so often in Colombia, we found ourselves scrambling to cope with the unforeseen.

In the first place, due to a major storm, electricity was shut off for most of the weekend that she stayed in our home. Poor Elizabeth never did get a hot meal at our house.

The baptism was scheduled, as before, to take place at the Baptist church in La Milagrosa on a Sunday, mid-afternoon. The church doors were opened for us only a half hour before starting time. Once inside, we saw that because of the storm the water had been shut off in that barrio and the tank held only about a foot or two of water. Harold would have to get creative in dunking.

Then we faced a problem of a different kind. For the previous baptism we had used the white gowns of the Baptist church for our female candidates. The male candidates wore pants and white shirts but we had assured the women there would be thick white gowns to cover them.

But, oh no! The gowns were missing. Loaned out.

It was a half hour before the service. I looked around. I saw Mariela who was a good sport and lived not too far away.

"Mariela, do you have a nightgown or housecoat that might be suitable to use?" She and I hopped into our jeep and raced down the hill to her home.

We looked through her nightgowns and both started giggling. "Now, really," I teased, "to think a good Christian has such see-through clothes and sexy nightgowns!"

We stopped giggling when we saw that time was speeding along. There were just minutes before the service would start.

We then searched through the closets in all the Sunday School rooms at our church and found two ancient white robes, yellowed with age, possibly old choir gowns from a bygone time.

"The women will look like grannies in these!"

"Well, at least they'll be modest."

We breathed great sighs of relief and dashed back with our booty to the Baptist church all the while wondering, *Now, will Elizabeth think us horribly unorganized?*

There, we found another challenge. All the light bulbs over the baptistery were burned out. Harold gave some pesos to a young man who ran to the corner store to buy new bulbs. The congregation patiently waited in the pews while men climbed on a ladder to install the new bulbs.

The service got underway about thirty-five minutes later than planned. No one complained.

And Elizabeth from Cali? She sat back, smiled and blessed us, accepting all the glitches as commonplace. She had lived so many decades in Colombia that nothing could surprise her. People whispered, "She is more Colombian than the Colombians."

29   Your documents, please

"It's time to renew our visas. We've been here a year now, hard to believe." Not just adults, but every person over seven years of age needed an identity card.

Together with Matthew and Rebecca we trundled off down the hill toward the DAS office, *Departamento Administrativo de Seguridad*, responsible for the country's intelligence and counter-intelligence. The building was cool and airy with a broad interior patio and green shutters open to the street.

"*Buenos dias*, we're here to renew our visas. These are the documents you asked us to bring at the last visit."

The middle-aged woman behind the desk wore a smart suit and a smile. "You have only two photos each?"

"Well, yes. That's what you asked for. See, you wrote it all down for us on this paper."

"Oh yes," more smiles, "but today you need four."

Groan.

"For now, then, step over here. We'll take each of your fingerprints. Come back next week with the photos."

Back in the jeep, Harold exhaled, "Next week they'll ask for some documents they've never asked for before. I know it! It took months of this kind of business last year to get ownership papers for the jeep."

I agreed. "It sure would be nice if there were a ready-made list of requirements. But since they keep changing the rules—"

Over the following weeks we got to know the woman at the DAS office and greeted her by name, Sandra.

That fall Andy had turned seven and needed to apply for his

identity card, his *cédula*. For his birthday party I made a cake in the shape of a rocket. It sat on the launching pad with red icing as fire under the rocket. I was going to write Canada in red icing on the rocket but all his school friends were American and so he insisted on me writing USA instead. The rest of the family protested but it was Andy's cake.

Andy with his rocket cake.

I went alone to apply for his card since Sandra at the DAS office knew our family. She greeted me with a smile and produced the documents.

"Here are the cards for Andrew," she said. "They need to be signed."

"He can't sign his own name," I explained. "He hasn't learned cursive writing yet."

She smiled.

"Then you write his signature for him. In BIG letters. You know, like a seven-year-old would do."

I could hardly wait to report when I got home.

"Harold! The government of Colombia asked me to forge a signature on a document for its own use. Amazing!"

By October we still had not been issued our renewed visas. At the beginning of the visa process, DAS had taken our passports and given us a *salvoconducta*, a safe-passage document to carry in our wallets, nothing more than a piece of paper stamped with an expiry date.

Possibly DAS procedures were taking extra-long because of heightened tensions in the country. That fall, security measures throughout the country were increased. Wherever we drove in the city we saw soldiers and guns on the streets. Driving to church, going for groceries, these routine trips were often interrupted by stops at military checkpoints.

A nation-wide strike meant school and other activities were briefly cancelled. Everyone stayed indoors to avoid trouble. Buses were burned, bridges destroyed. Newspapers and radio warned Colombians their country was on the brink of revolution.

Harold and I longed to get away. In our previous life in Canada we had the custom of going away at least once a year for a romantic weekend without kids. Now we hadn't been away together for almost two years.

A friend recommended Santa Fé de Real, about an hour and a half from Medellín. We farmed out the kids to friends' homes and eagerly set off.

CONTRA LA CARESTIA
Y LA REPRESIÓN
21 OCT PARO C. NAL
COMBATIVO Y REVOLUCIONA-
RIO, A LA CALLE U.D.R.

Graffiti inciting revolution, a regular sight in the barrio.

But first we stopped at the DAS office to see if possibly our visas had arrived. What a surprise. They had changed their entire staff (was it for security?) and so Sandra, who knew us well and had done all our paperwork, was no longer there. No one else knew us.

"Please, can you check if there are new *salvoconductas* for us?"

"Why do you need those?" No smiles.

"Our passports are still in Bogotá getting stamped with new visas. We are going to travel outside the city and all we have now are these expired *salvoconductas*. Can you check please if there are new ones for us?"

"We don't have time for this today. Come back another time."

Back in the jeep my risk-loving husband said, "We'll take our chances. If we don't get stopped, we'll be okay."

All we had in our wallets were our temporary *salvoconductas*, now dog-eared, stating we could stay in Colombia until September 24.

But now it was October 11. We hoped to get to Santa Fé with no military checkpoints stopping us along the way. Praying for safe passage, we set off down the road.

We tried to enjoy the trip, yet it was hard to relax when at each bend of the road we held our breath hoping there would be no military checkpoint to hold us up. When we arrived at the little country inn, Hostería Real, we breathed a sigh of relief. We'd come all the way with no incident. Thank God!

After settling into our modest room, feeling triumphant about getting there so easily, I suggested, "Why don't we go see the town of Santa Fé just up the road from here? It's historic and they say it's quaint and beautiful."

We had not gone far down the road when—what was this? A military checkpoint. A large group of people seemed to be marching with big banners strung across the road. It looked like a protest march for indigenous people.

Soldiers on guard near Santa Fé de Antioquia.

The highway was crawling with soldiers. They lined the roadsides and commanded the hillsides overlooking the road, military rifles in hand.

"Stop! Get out!" We obeyed and stepped down to the road. They vigorously frisked Harold. Then they rummaged through the camera bag and my purse. I felt strangely calm. Just young guys, I thought, fulfilling their eighteen-month compulsory service.

"Your documents!"

Harold slowly reached to his pocket. One by one he took out cards, any cards, until he'd shown them all his important papers.

"No, no, not those! Just show us your ID card, la *cédula*."

Just what we didn't have.

Harold spread out his much-creased, past-due *salvoconducta*. "We're in process. Getting our visas."

The soldier stared at the paper and rubbed his chin. Then he gave a sideways glance at the other soldiers. Finally, he shrugged and motioned us to pass through the checkpoint.

We breathed a sigh and climbed back into the jeep.

As we pulled forward I said, "Harold, when we come back we'll have to face the other side of the *retén* and those guys might not be so lenient."

Then, to my surprise, my husband embraced caution. While still in sight of the checkpoint, he swung the jeep around and we drove by the soldiers on the return side. He drove slowly but did not stop.

I stuck my head out the window, gave a big smile to the soldiers and called out cheerily, "For us tourists it's better to come back tomorrow."

We were waved through.

Back in our humble room with the wooden beds and hard cotton mattresses we finally relaxed. "Let's have a cold drink on this little balcony outside our window."

We sat down, took a sip, looked up and saw on the ledge above us a tiny jungle owl. He winked at us and seemed to say, "Be wise. Stay put."

We enjoyed the whole weekend, feeling no need to venture beyond the beautiful grounds of the country inn.

30 The Christmas spirit

That year, 1988, would be our fourth Christmas away from Canada and we wanted to make good memories with our children. In mid-December we took the kids to a concert by the Colombian Symphony Orchestra. What a rare treat. Walking into the concert hall was like stepping into a time capsule. It completely shut out the traffic noise, the buses backfiring, the gunshots, the endless honking of horns. We settled in, sat back and enjoyed the New World Symphony by Dvořák, Harold's favorite composer. I was transported to a different world. And, oh, the emotions expressed, the beauty!

We promised ourselves we would return often, but it turned out to be the only time we went to Medellín's concert hall.

On December 17 we invited the church youth for a Christmas party at our house. Becky and I prepared meatballs, special cheeses, a pineapple-cherry nut bread and hot chocolate. As the youth arrived, I greeted each one in the traditional way. Freddy came too and looked cheerful. Maybe things were turning out all right for his family.

As soon as they were settled in, I left Harold, Matthew and Becky to entertain the group and I retreated to the bedroom. I usually loved working with these young people, but I recognized a chance to escape to be alone. I craved that, especially during a people-filled season like Christmas.

I was deep into Agatha Christie's autobiography that day and found it fascinating—like her books. I admired how it was written, too, because she gives the impression of rambling on and yet it's well-planned, careful rambling. I really did miss the world of writing. When would I write again?

December raced ahead in a hectic fashion. The next week we invited Harold's Spanish tutor for supper. "I am thinking about becoming a Christian, like you people," he told us over a plate of mashed potatoes, *good* mashed potatoes this time, and chicken.

The next day a traveling preacher arrived for three nights and I put him up in Matthew's room. Matthew set up a foamie on the floor in the boys' bunk room. Between meals I set the sewing machine on the dining room table and kept busy sewing costumes for the kids for the school plays and the drama at church.

"Watch yourself," Harold warned. "You don't want to get sick for Christmas."

I pouted. "How do you watch your health with guests every day? And then on December 29 we have strangers arriving, houseguests for six weeks. It was very nice of them to offer to help build the church but why, oh why, is it assumed that all missionaries love to entertain and have houseguests without end?"

When we first heard an American couple was coming here after Christmas to work on the church construction, we said, "Hallelujah!"

On the other hand, they would be staying in our home and that meant my time and energies would be shared. What should take priority, I wondered: the children's needs, special guest meals, church duties, family time, or keeping marital harmony?

"Who in North America," I wondered out loud, "would consider keeping strangers for six weeks in a house with no guest room and four children and the wife with some kind of chronic illness?"

I was feeling sorry for myself, for sure. Not a good place to be. So, I turned back to the sewing machine to finish the costumes for a rabbi and a prisoner in the church drama.

The next day I cleared away the sewing machine to make room for another project. Soon the table was covered with wash basins and pans full of popcorn. I was making poppycock to put into pretty gift bags for all the church people. It took hours but was economical and I did want to give something to these dear people who were sure to have a sparse celebration.

Popcorn to make poppycock.

Upstairs, hidden away, all our children's gifts were wrapped including special treats from grandparents and aunts and uncles. It looked like we were set for a happy season.

But of course, life never stands still.

The next day we rushed Becky to the clinic with what looked to be appendicitis. After numerous tests, it was diagnosed as an inflammation from tropical bacteria so, thankfully, no surgery was needed. Then the next day her little dog Mitzi got itchy bumps all over so Harold hunted down a vet who saw her and gave the right medication.

As Becky recovered, Harold arranged an afternoon soccer game with the church guys. Off he went to a soccer field where they would meet for the game.

Meanwhile, the sky opened up and rain poured down in sheets. Rain overflowed the eavestroughs and seeped inside the house. Soon it was running down the stairs into the living room. What a mess! I got bucket and pail out and the little boys helped sop up the water with rags.

Then suddenly there was Harold. The jeep pulled up and out poured the whole youth group.

"Can't play soccer in this rain!"

I cast about looking for what snack I could serve them. Meanwhile, the youth urged Matthew to play piano for them. None of them could play, yet they loved music. They gathered round him at the keyboard and kept exclaiming what a novelty it was. I smiled. What a change from Canada where so many play piano. At least so it seemed when I was growing up. After a few lessons when I was young, I had refused to take any more.

"I'm not learning piano!" I told my distraught parents. "Everyone plays piano. I won't do it!" All four of my sisters became great pianists, two earning their ARCT degrees, but I never learned to play. So now, of course, I wanted all my children to learn the keyboard.

While Matthew played, I rummaged in the freezer. My loving parents had sent money to buy a freezer since they could not imagine a family of six having guests and doing ministry without one. Thanks to baking I had stashed there, I was able to rustle up a decent snack for the youth group. Quick breads and hot chocolate. Just right for a rainy day.

The church youth in our *sala*.

The next morning, I wished I could just stay in bed.

I lay back and told the ceiling, "I was created to be an upper-class woman in the Victorian era. I'm at my best with a leisurely breakfast in bed and an interesting book before facing the day."

But the ceiling took no notice. Neither did anyone else.

Instead, like most days, I fumbled my way out of bed around 6:30, packed several lunches, filled several thermoses and then tried to civilly answer Harold's inevitable question, "Why is the bread always frozen?"

When the holidays arrived, Harold bought a splendid 1000-piece jigsaw puzzle of a North American village nestled in snowy hills. It was a delight, providing hours of nostalgic Christmas memories. I revelled in the change of pace.

31   The pig that climbed stairs

The church pig in Medellín was not like the pig that author Beatrix Potter kept at Hill Top Farm in England. Beatrix always feared her pig would climb the stairs to the second floor.

Our pig? Well, if only!

Christmas was still a long way off when the church members told us excitedly, "We've bought a baby pig! It was cheap now because it's so small, but we're keeping it where it will be fed. *Y que maravilla*, at Christmas the church will have a nice fat pig to roast for us all. *Una lechona.*"

That was in September. A month or so later I was surprised to discover this pig of promise during a home visit to a church member.

I went with Elsa to visit a young mother with a new baby. Both parents were regulars at church but I had not seen their home. Maybe the word "home" is too grand for the rooms they lived in. It was a good thing Elsa guided me there because I would not have found my way on my own.

First, we stepped off the street into a dark entryway. Concrete steps led down into a dim interior. At the landing another set of stairs led deeper into the earth.

We came out four storeys below ground on a narrow walkway that ran around a central courtyard. The only light came from far above, through the square opening at the top of the courtyard. Clotheslines hung with laundry between the walkway posts. Elsa knocked at one of the closed doors along the walkway.

It was opened by the young mother who welcomed us nervously with the customary kiss on the cheek. In her arms was the baby. She stepped out into the walkway with him so that we could see his face in the daylight. A beautiful baby boy!

Inside, the home was dark. There were three rooms but only the one room facing the walkway had a window. The other rooms were dark as caves. I marvelled at how neat the young mother kept her little home in what was to me a frightening place.

We were in an underground apartment complex. Till then I hadn't known that thousands with no better alternative, lived inside the mountains of Medellín. No wonder the people hailed drug lord Pablo Escobar as a hero. In some poor barrios he had built entire housing complexes above ground. To the rest of the world he was evil and ruthless but some of the poor of Medellín honoured him as a saint.

Outside the window, beyond lines strung with laundry, I saw a pig rooting on the ground in the central courtyard.

"Yes," she pointed, "that's the church pig. He's getting nice and fat, no? He gets the scraps from all the families here."

As Christmas and New Year approached the church made plans for a special gathering. I was distracted, though, by news I read in the newspaper. Two vans carrying mail into the city from the airport were intercepted. Two complete airmail shipments had disappeared. Which cards, letters or gifts had gone missing from our friends and family? We never did discover what we had missed and had a fine Christmas until I remembered the chocolates.

"That's what I'm missing! Now I know. That box of homemade chocolates that Betty Poettker's been sending from Morden each year. Stolen, I guess. I hope someone's enjoying them and thinks good thoughts of dear Betty."

One morning a few days before New Year's Eve, the phone rang for Harold.

"Would you please, dear brother, come with your jeep and help us get the pig to the church?"

Harold left in the jeep, picked up three young men waiting for him at the church and together they set out into the maze of barrio streets. At the entrance to the underground apartment block they said, "Come. We'll show you."

Down they went, down three flights of dark stairs. There in the dim light stood a big gray and pink pig, rooting in the mud.

"Please, brother, we don't know how to get this pig out of here. No one knows how. How can we get a pig up all those stairs?"

Harold looked at the pig that had grown large and fat. Where to take hold of a chubby pig to lead him up a dark stairway?

During Harold's boyhood on the farm he had handled pigs and knew that a pig has a mind of its own and is not easily led where it doesn't want to go.

Back up the stairs he went to the jeep where he found a length of rope. Then back down the flights of stairs. Harold and the young men went into the pen and pressed the pig into a corner. With rope in hand, Harold swung a leg over the pig's back and tied the rope around its chest. Then another rope around its middle in front of the back legs. By now his jeans, shirt and shoes were spattered with muck.

With some pulling in front and others pushing behind, they struggled that poor, reluctant creature up the first flight of stairs. They stopped to breathe and then tackled the next flight and the next. At last out on the street, they hoisted the pig into the back of our jeep and drove to the churchyard.

Harold brings the pig to church.

The grand feast with roasted pig was planned for New Year's Eve.

On December 30, Ken Flaming and his wife Sara arrived at our house from Oklahoma to help with the church construction. I liked them immediately. They were fun and completely relaxed, putting me at ease as well.

"They are the most wonderful couple," I wrote home. "We're very encouraged having them. They'll be in our home a month or six weeks and already on their first day Ken built a backboard in the patio to mount the basketball hoop we gave the boys for Christmas. Then he built shelves in the maid's room, which is really Harold's study, and our only storage room. The Flamings are so easy to have around. Because foods are so different here, we've agreed that I will do the cooking and Sara do the cleanup."

On December 31st, the Flamings joined our church for the New Year's celebration. It was a night when traditionally all Latin America is out on the street dancing and getting drunk. The church planned a fiesta for that evening so that our members and new converts could enjoy a safe and healthy New Year's Eve.

The church was packed, the crowd spilling out onto the green space outside the railings. Everyone was there, babies to seniors. The extraordinary program included singing, storytelling, testimonials, a puppet show and a slide show of the church's *campamento* held earlier that year. Seeing themselves on the screen, people poked each other, teased and chuckled together. At midnight a communion service carried us all into the year 1989 in a great spirit of fellowship.

On this festive occasion the whole pig was roasted jungle style. The feast gave so much joy to the church families. Not accustomed to generous portions of meat, the people enjoyed their full plates with great gratitude.

Harold and I were handed choice plates heaped with what Colombians consider a treat—large strips of crispy pork rind, *chicharron*. We hadn't eaten this before. Harold, always up to a food challenge, dug in.

I offered mine to Freddy who took it with a big grin and said, "O, *Señora* Doroti, may God bless you for your generosity!"

And God did. He surely did.

 ## 32   Kidnapping

On Tuesday, January 4, 1989 the phone rang.

"Have you heard? Two missionaries were kidnapped near Cali yesterday."

It was the news we all dreaded hearing. Kidnapping had become a popular way for armed groups to raise money. *The Washington Post* reported 709 kidnappings took place in Colombia during 1988.

On hearing the news, we froze but then wanted the details.

"They're with the Gospel Missionary Union. Two American men. One was their mission leader, Roy Libby from Bogotá. The other man was from Medellín here, Richard Grover."

"Dick Grover! That's terrible! We know him. His daughter's in Matthew's class at school. What happened?"

We learned the missionaries were together with their Colombian pastors holding their annual convention at a *finca* outside Cali. Ten guerrillas dressed in military uniforms drove onto the property. They went straight for these two *gringos*, taking the men at gunpoint. So far there was no word as to whether the guerrillas had contacted anyone with their demands.

"What about Grover's family?" I asked.

"The wife and daughter hadn't gone to Cali for the meetings. They stayed back in Medellín. We don't know what the plan is. Usually, of course, the mission gets the family out of the country pretty quick."

I blurted out, "We have our mission convention on a *finca* near Cali, too. This coming weekend."

"I wouldn't go if I were you."

I hung up and wondered what we would do.

The annual convention of our Mennonite Brethren conference of churches was to be held at La Cumbre, thirty kilometers north of Cali. This rural property had been owned by the Mennonite Brethren for decades and had previously served as school grounds. Now a rustic dormitory building stood there, along with a chapel and a viable coffee plantation under the care of a *majordomo* and his family. We had never yet seen the place, a day's drive from Medellín.

The scheduled convention would include our Colombian pastors with their families together with missionaries and their families. Following that convention, the plan was for a conference in English for missionaries and their families at the same *finca*.

We had put off deciding whether we would attend because Harold was deep into the construction at the church. He was in charge of the overall project while Ken Flaming worked on the aspects that called for experienced craftmanship. Unfortunately, Ken was often being harassed by neighbourhood boys throwing rocks and bottles at him, shouting, "Go home, Yankee." Ken, a gentle soul, carried on quietly working.

The youth from the church, on the other hand, held Ken in high regard and became his good friends. Ken and Sara were easy-going house guests but they didn't speak Spanish. We worried about going to the convention and leaving them on their own in Medellín. We hadn't decided yet whether to go or stay home.

When the kids came home from school, they dropped their backpacks and scrambled to the table for their afternoon snack of cookies and hot chocolate. I broke the news of the kidnapping.

"Her dad was kidnapped?" Matthew asked. "She's in my class. So that's why she wasn't there today."

"Yes, it's true," I sighed. "In Cali. The principal, Mr. Rempel, called to tell us."

The chairs scraped on the tile as the kids pulled them up to the table. It seemed unreal to have the usual afternoon snack as though this day was no different from every other day. The kids looked at me to see what else I would add but I was lost in thought. I poured hot chocolate from the metal pitcher into assorted mugs.

"Cali," Andy said. "Isn't that where we're going, too?"

"Not sure. Not sure yet. Dad might need to stay to do construction work."

"But we want to play with Aaron and Silas. We never see them."

"Do we still have to practise piano today?" asked Rebecca.

"It's Wednesday. Yes, of course," I answered distractedly. "Tomorrow's your lesson."

And just like that we were back to the mundane details of life as if nothing had happened. Thursday was the day the piano teacher came to the house to give the children lessons. His name was Hector, a young medical student fluent in English, making money on the side to get through medical school. He had been offered an internship in a large New York hospital but turned it down.

"Why go to New York?" his advisors had said. "In the emergency rooms in Medellín you'll get more surgical practice than anywhere else, the same as in a war zone."

So, he stayed. When I saw his hands resting on the keyboard next to our child's hands I sometimes wondered which bomb fragments those fingers had extracted that day and which gunshot wounds they had sewn up.

At supper we all prayed earnestly that the kidnapped men would be returned to their families.

After supper the phone rang again.

"We're coordinating meals for Dick Grover's family. His wife, Charleen and daughter are still here in Medellín. Haven't heard any more news yet, so it's a hard time. Would you take a turn at taking a meal to their home?"

"Of course!"

Two days later Rebecca and I loaded a casserole and other goodies into the back of the jeep. "I don't know what to say to them," I confided to Rebecca on the way. "What do you say? It's different from visiting a sick person or even a family where someone died. It's just totally different."

"They don't know where he is—"

"No. No one knows where he is. We need to keep praying. No one knows what'll happen to him."

At the house, a low-roofed, modest home, we rang the bell. Other missionaries, staying there round the clock, greeted us. They whisked away the food and then we sat on wooden chairs in a wide hallway, speaking in low voices with other visitors who had come to offer moral support. We didn't see the wife or daughter. They were being kept in seclusion for their own safety.

On the way home Rebecca asked, "Mom, are we still going to Cali?"

"I don't know, sweetheart. We're still deciding if we'll go. Maybe only Dad will go."

When we got home, Harold was on the phone with John Savoia in Cali. I heard him agree that we would go to the conference. Okay, get ready. The kids were excited but I was sceptical.

The next day, a Saturday afternoon January 7, 1989, I wrote in my journal.

"Decided yesterday that Harold and I and the three youngest will drive to Cali tomorrow. I quickly washed three loads of laundry this morning—moved all the clotheslines out from under the roof, hoping it dries so I can iron. Matthew is staying home here with the Flamings—I'm so grateful. It's good for both parties. Matt wants to stay and get ready for exams next week. He can translate for Ken and Sara. They've been wonderful, very relaxing to have as houseguests.

"Tomorrow we leave for Cali. People have expressed concern although we'll be north of Cali and the kidnapping was south. In fact, the Gospel Missionary Union phoned and urged our mission team to stay home. However, we have all agreed we'll meet there."

No word had come in since the kidnapping and that was worrying. Were the men still alive?

The phone rang that night.

"Listen, the kidnappers have now sent a note. It says they will kill the two Americans if more Colombians are extradited to the States. They demanded the release of that drug dealer, Carlos Lehder, who's supposed to serve a life sentence in the States."

"That's not good. Not good at all."

"You still driving down Cali way?"

"We're still going. Our team seems to think it'll be okay."

"Well, be careful."

The next morning we loaded the three youngest kids into the jeep for the seven-hour drive to Cali. Matthew and the Flamings assured us they would manage fine.

It was thrilling to leave the city behind. The Medellín-Cali highway twists its way along mountainsides with breathtaking views. One section of the highway runs along the arête of a mountaintop, the land falling away steeply on *both* sides of the road. I kept holding my breath hoping to help the jeep stay in our narrow lane.

Because of the kidnapping, I packed differently for this trip and for every trip we made after that. I took my make-up bag out of my purse and packed it away in a suitcase. In its place I stowed my Bible, pen and notepad. In case we'd be kidnapped, hurried away into the jungle, I was prepared with the essentials.

The *finca* at La Cumbre turned out to be a beautiful grassy acreage overlooking a mountainside smothered in coffee plants and banana trees. We met many of our Colombian pastors and their families for the first time. What an exuberant mix of calls and hugs as we greeted each other. Everyone had driven, bussed or motorcycled in from various barrios in the major cities of Cali and Bogotá. Plus, there were workers from the remote Chocó region along the coast as well.

The finca at La Cumbre.

A pastor brings his family to La Cumbre.

Becky and I would be sleeping on the women's side of the building with the pastors' wives and children in a large dormitory room filled with metal bunk beds.

"You want to sleep on top?" I asked her.

"Oh, yes."

I sat down on the mattress of the lower bunk and blurted out in English to Becky, "How will I ever sleep on this? It didn't give even an inch when I sat down! It's rock hard."

Then across the room I overheard a Colombian pastor's wife exclaim to another in Spanish, "Aren't these cotton mattresses just wonderful, sister?"

"Thank God," the other woman answered. "So much better than those smelly straw mattresses we had until now, full of bugs."

Ah well, I decided, *not so bad after all.*

Downstairs we met for rousing singing in the chapel. Everyone avoided talk of kidnapping but I noticed small knots of men and women whispering and looking over to where I sat with our fair-haired children.

When night fell everyone found their beds and the lights were turned off. The countryside was steeped in a thick blackness broken only by faint stars above.

I lay on the hard mattress and listened. The night air stretched thin. The chirping of crickets and the barking of a distant dog did not comfort me. My ears strained to detect the slightest sound. Was that a car engine in the distance? My muscles tensed. Was the engine getting louder and closer? Or was it dying away in the opposite direction?

Oh Lord, let it pass us by.

I had no plan in mind. An invasion of gunmen was such a scary prospect I decided I would deal with it if and when it happened.

The next morning when the sun shone it seemed impossible to imagine violence and terror breaking in on the beauty of this countryside. In the women's washroom, it was fun to joke with the pastors' wives about the icy cold showers. I pretended I could take the unheated water like they did and not like the wimpy foreigner I actually was.

I chatted with the wives of the Colombian pastors, trying to remember their names and where each one was from. I enjoyed the warm camaraderie of eating our meals on simple benches at long wooden tables. The sight of our children sitting with the children of the Colombian pastors and enjoying every bite of the Colombian food warmed my heart.

Meals were simple but good. Breakfast consisted of a bun with cheese and a bowl of sweet *café con leche*. The other two meals were fried plantains and rice. Or beans. Or *sancocho*, the Cali version of chicken soup. Drinks were handed out in coloured plastic cups, two-thirds cup per person no matter how hot or thirsty people were. No refills. The drink was usually *aqua panela*, cane sugar dissolved in water, or *avena*, a drink made with oatmeal flour, water, a touch of cinnamon and a splash of milk.

Following the retreat, we missionaries planned to stay at the *finca* for our own separate meetings. It was our one chance to be together with our co-workers from other cities.

"No way!" the Colombian leaders insisted. "It's too dangerous for you foreigners to stay any longer in this rural location. Too great a risk."

We finally relented only when we realized that if anything happened it would place too great an onus on the Colombian leadership.

Kids' lunch at La Cumbre.

But where would we hold our meetings? It was disappointing to drive down the mountain into the sweltering city of Cali where we squeezed into the homes of our Cali team members and held our missionary meetings indoors rather than on the beautiful hillsides.

When we got back to Medellín we called around. "Still no word about the two kidnapped men?"

"No. Nothing. But their families have been flown to Ecuador. They're waiting it out there, hoping the men will be released soon."

No word from the kidnappers. That was a little scary. Did it mean they just wanted to take foreigners and do away with them? All the North Americans we knew were feeling nervous.

Fortunately, less than two months later both men were freed and reunited with their families in Ecuador. From there they flew home to the States. We all thanked God and breathed a sigh of relief.

An official statement said no ransom had been paid. Mission agencies are strictly opposed to paying ransom demands. But the relatives of missionaries are not tied to these mission rules. Who knew what had happened? And, certainly none of us who worked in Colombia, none of us looking over our shoulders in fear every day, certainly none of us would judge them either way.

These two men were the fortunate ones. In the future, other missionaries we knew in this country would disappear, never to return.

33   The fridge is not an emergency

On our return to Medellín after the meetings in Cali, the church elders asked us to visit Magda to straighten out a delicate issue. Usually our visits to homes were related to family conflicts, extra-marital affairs or financial need. But this was money trouble of a different kind.

Harold and I drove to the Salvador barrio to visit Magda one gray sultry afternoon, rain falling in sheets. "How can we talk with these people about money troubles?" I asked Harold. "In their eyes we're rich foreigners. It must seem a farce to them."

Magda was tall and broad-shouldered. She rarely smiled and wore the look of a fighter in the corner of the ring ready to take on her opponent—the rest of humanity. She'd survived years of civil war and not a scratch on her! She stood tough and unbending.

She lived in a shared apartment on the second floor of a house that stood on a main road running through the centre of the barrio and on up the hill. Every ten minutes or so a bus chugged its way up the road, passing another on its way down, squealing the brakes and belching diesel fumes.

We parked the jeep on the side of the road with one set of tires up on the sidewalk to keep it out of the way of the buses. We knocked on the metal door at the bottom of her stairway, making sure we knocked in the polite Colombian way, slowly and deliberately. The quick rap, rap, rap of a North American knock shows impatience and is very rude.

Magda led the way upstairs to the *sala* from which doors led off to bedrooms and bathroom. This main room held a few chairs, a settee, a wooden table, the narrow stove, the sink and the fridge.

The air was heavy with the smell of damp clothing. She had done her laundry and every surface was hung with some garment to dry. Towels on the railing along the stairs, socks across the lamp top. She lifted a shirt from a chair back and motioned for Harold to sit. With her usual brusqueness she pushed a space open for me on the settee and indicated I was to sit there.

She set a metal pitcher of water to boil on the stove, then tugged a wooden chair across the floor for herself. She sat down on the edge of it to avoid leaning against the pale flowered skirt that hung to dry across its back.

I decided to lay the groundwork with pleasantries and asked, "Have you been keeping well?"

"I've had a very hard time. The fridge did not work well, you see, and the weather was hot. It wasn't fair that I should have a poor fridge."

So, she'd guessed why we came.

"No, surely," I agreed. "It's a hard thing to have no fridge when the weather's hot."

"There was money in the church. I asked Bruno and he said the *ancianos* had some funds in the bank."

"Yes, Magda. The church elders have a small fund."

"So, when I needed a fridge and when the money was there, then it seemed God wanted me to have a new fridge."

I nodded. "It must have seemed that way."

The water boiled and Magda stood to make coffee. We watched her pour the boiling water through a cloth bag that held coffee grounds. The pale coffee dripped through into a pot. She poured it back through the bag and repeated that twice. She poured the coffee into demitasse cups into which she stirred two teaspoons of sugar each, then handed us each a cup on a saucer. It was delicious.

"I'm very glad that you missionaries came here to Medellín," she said with her usual stern look. "Since you are here, everything is much better."

But buttering us up would not do.

"Well, we're glad to be back in Medellín after our trip to the conference in Cali. Imagine how surprised we were to hear that while we were away all the money of the *ancianos* had been spent."

The topic was warming up.

"Do you know why the *ancianos* keep a small fund on hand in the bank?" Harold asked.

"To help people, of course."

"Yes. That's right. For instance," Harold said, "Luis is in hospital doing very badly and his mother goes every day to see him. The bus costs money, right? And poor Carlos is up the mountain dying of cancer. His wife had to stop her job to stay home to take care of him. So how will they feed their children now if she can't work?"

"Everyone has their troubles, that's true," Magda conceded.

"The money you used for your fridge is not for fridges," Harold said. "The money in the *anciano* fund is to help people who are in real need. Sometimes they're desperate. Getting a better fridge is not what the money is for."

Silence. A stony look.

"The money will have to be repaid," Harold continued quietly. "The church needs to help those who are suffering."

Magda's face stiffened and her chin rose.

"I was suffering, *hermano*. I was suffering."

"The money can be repaid over time. You can give a little bit each month until it's paid back."

Two weeks later the church held one of their nighttime prayer vigils. Because the service would go on past midnight, only the few and the faithful would attend. Harold and I arrived early and pulled the benches into a U-shape to make the meeting more intimate.

Among those who walked in the door was Magda, striding in, wearing her thick white pumps and pale flowered skirt, her chin held high. After an hour of singing and reading Scripture, the prayer time began. Along with the other women, she rose from her bench, knelt down on the concrete floor with her elbows resting on the bench.

I knelt, too. The rough concrete dug its pointy peaks into the flesh of my knees. After a half hour on my knees I yearned to get up.

I snuck a peek over at Magda. I had to admire her. She was still beside the bench, her old bare knees pressed into the concrete, her lips moving. Was she praying for the sick and dying? Thanking for her fridge? Praying for the missionaries to change their mind about repaying the money?

"Dear God," I prayed. "Why is being a missionary so hard? How do we know if we're getting it right?"

 ## 34   I honk, you shoot

Harold jumped back into working hard on the construction of the church building. In between pastoral duties and supervising workers he often dashed about in the jeep to buy materials.

Harold unloads adobe brick at church before driving home for lunch.

One day while waiting for him to come home for lunch, I heard the jeep grind to a halt in our driveway. Harold fumbled with the key at the front door. When the door opened, he stood there ashen-faced.

"What's the matter?" I asked.

Then I moaned, "Oh no. You were robbed again—"

He shook his head then stumbled over to the sofa and sank down.

"Well, what then? What's happened?" I'd never before seen Harold so shaken up. He kept staring across the room in silence. He opened his mouth to speak, but instead, a great sigh escaped. Finally, he started in a low voice and the story came out bit by bit in his usual chop-dash style.

On his way home from construction he drove through a barrio he had been warned against. But it was a shortcut to home. Closely packed houses left little room for vehicles to pass each other.

He turned a sharp corner and saw ahead of him a red sports car parked right in the centre of the street. There was no way to get by. He stopped about fifty feet behind it.

Two men sat in the car. They took no notice of Harold. Their car was idling, so Harold thought if he let them know he was there they would move over to let him pass.

He tooted the horn, just two little beeps. Both men turned around and looked back. The driver opened his door and turned to look at Harold.

He shouted something.

Harold didn't understand what was shouted so he threw both hands in the air to show he didn't know what was meant.

The driver swung around in his seat, put one foot on the ground. In his hand was a gun aimed at Harold.

"I just sat there. Couldn't believe what I saw. Then he shot at me. I felt something but didn't know if they'd really hit me or not. Dropped down onto the front seat and waited. Didn't know what to expect. In a few seconds my foot came off the brake and the jeep started rolling. I looked up. They were gone. They must have figured they got me."

"So, they missed!"

"I got this."

He lifted his arm and I saw a splay of deep cuts running from the wrist to the elbow.

I gasped.

Glass pieces stared out of several of the gashes.

"My arm was on the open window. Bullet hit the bottom of the side mirror. Smashed to bits. These are pieces of the mirror. I was really lucky."

I set to work picking out the glass shards. Then I bandaged the cuts. Together we went out to inspect the jeep.

The mirror was shattered. In the chrome that lined the lower window edge ran a deep dent.

"Look at that!" I exclaimed. "The bullet passed just a fraction of an inch from where you were resting your elbow. Your left elbow could have been shattered. And you being left-handed, too. It could have been horrible."

The front door of the neighbour's house opened and the little Napoleon appeared. He strutted over.

"An accident?" he asked.

Harold explained.

"Drug dealers!" roared the little man. "In that barrio and in a sports car, it couldn't have been anything else. They probably thought you were checking them out. Or maybe they were just annoyed you were bothering them."

He continued on in his strident voice. "And, he expected you would be getting your own gun out, so he made sure he was first. Why didn't you get your gun out? Wasn't it under the seat?"

"No, I don't own a gun."

"No, no! What a mistake!" he roared. "In Medellín you can't be without a gun. I would never be without a gun. I'm a retired military doctor, you know, and am always watchful. Why, even when I sit on my balcony reading the newspaper, I have my gun with me. If I would see any suspicious looking character on the street—poom! I would shoot first and ask questions later."

He leaned into Harold's face with a wry grin, "Like in your Old West, no?"

And, like in the Old West, there was no reporting the incident and no investigation—these things just happened.

 35   Looks like a church

With the untiring help of Ken Flaming, the arched windows and the arched double doors were installed in the new church building. It was finally looking like a church and not an empty lot.

Ken Flaming and a Colombian worker construct
the front face of the church.

We couldn't have done it without you! The church youth thank Sara and
Ken Flaming.

On Ken's last Sunday everyone crowded around him to thank him,
and admire his workmanship on the new stairway he was completing
to finally connect the old basement meeting room with the new
sanctuary at street level. It was good to see Ken grinning and accepting
pats on the back from the church men.

That Sunday, too, Magda approached Anna Enns and me and
announced in her strident voice, "Next to God, the arrival of you
people is the best thing ever to happen to us."

I blinked. That was Magda talking? I guess she forgave us for
insisting she pay back the church money she had used to buy a new
fridge. Small miracles.

High points often preceded new challenges. That very Sunday
the membership met to discuss what beliefs our church held on the
complex topic of the Holy Spirit. People wanted clarity because a

strange young fellow had appeared in the neighbourhood preaching on street corners, proclaiming that complete healing could come to everyone who prayed with enough faith.

Fortunately, the church elders were united in thought with Harold who had the moral support, too, of Galen, and of Albert Enns. So, Harold's job of explaining these thoughts to the congregation was made easier than expected.

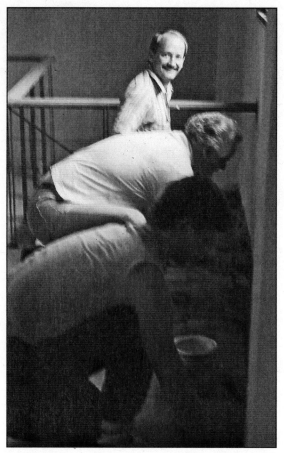

From the top: Galen, Henry Schmidt and Fred Leonard paint baseboards in the new sanctuary the day before the inauguration.

Later, a board member called me. "Doroti, you know how in the past many things have gone wrong in this church. People did very strange things thinking they were following the Spirit. So, what Harold explained about the Holy Spirit was a tremendous victory. I want you to know it is a landmark in the history of the church."

I passed those comments on to Harold and that cheered him up. He needed cheering because pressure was growing to complete the church construction. The elders aimed to have the building complete a week before Easter. Easter week was a big occasion on the Colombian calendar and they wanted to use the new sanctuary that week for special services.

Easter came very early that year.

"We would like the first service in the new sanctuary to be held on Palm Sunday, March 19," the elders announced. "Then during the Easter week we'll hold special meetings each evening."

That decision put a fire under Harold. He worked day and evening to reach the goal. And he reached it with help from friends.

Special visitors arrived to celebrate the opening day. Henry Schmidt, professor of missions from the MB Seminary in California, joined us with his wife Elvera. It was special for us to host them in our home as honoured guests, but more than that, Harold and Henry had grown up in the same rural area and had a shared past. Henry's task, as official representative from the North American office, was to inaugurate the building but that did not stop him from pitching in and getting his hands dirty. When he saw Harold scrambling to finish construction details, he happily picked up a paintbrush on Saturday so that all would be ready for the inauguration ceremony the next day.

Linda baked and decorated beautiful large cakes for the inauguration event. The church ladies supplied drinks. For this occasion, the colourful plastic cups would not be enough so we bought disposable cups for the extra crowd. I sewed a large colourful cloth banner that was ready just in time. We mounted it on the wall of the new sanctuary.

Our first service in the new sanctuary, Sunday, March 19, 1989.

The beautiful new church.

It was exciting to see the church people enter the sanctuary for the first time through the arched double doorway. Inside, the high corrugated roof and the concrete tile floor brought a pleasant coolness to the interior. Benches were packed with an even bigger turnout than expected, leaving standing room only.

What excitement! The strumming of guitars, the beating of tambourines. Children and adults sang and clapped with delight, their loud celebration reverberating off the open ceiling.

The emotion of this fresh start spilled over into the community. A special outreach campaign was held in the new sanctuary at which the evangelist Albert Enns drew crowds with his captivating stories.

Though Harold had worked day and night for weeks to get ready for the dedication of the new church building, he couldn't rest. Instead, he coordinated the logistics of these special meetings and, every day for the two weeks of the campaign, he mounted megaphones on the jeep at 4 p.m. and drove around the barrio with other members announcing that evening's gathering.

These meetings brought about twenty-five new converts into our church from the community. That was an exciting result and we worked to link these new people with small groups of members that met in homes during the week, between Sundays.

One afternoon I stood in the church alone looking at the coloured glass windows. They took me back to the small town of Vineland, Ontario where my father had been pastor when I was a teenager. One of my favorite activities was to borrow a key from the front closet in our parsonage home, cross the road to the church when I knew it was empty, unlock the heavy oak door and wander the aisles of the sanctuary while the setting sun lit the arched stained-glass windows.

Sometimes I stood in the aisle and sang hymns aloud and heard them echo off the wooden beams.

In this new sanctuary I was too shy to sing aloud as there were workers below in the basement. But I whispered to the space, "You have stirred nostalgia in me. You give me a sense of comfort and of home."

I hoped our Colombians, too, would find here a place of beauty and peace, a refuge drawing them into the true sanctuary of the Divine.

36   Restless

It was Saturday and Harold left for a meeting with the church elders. I thought, *Wouldn't it be lovely to find time to write again—to send off an article to a magazine back home.* Instead, it was time to write another letter for our supporters. I sat down with Matthew to discuss graphics for our newsletter, *The Siebert Herald*.

Under the heading "Prayer Needed" I added a request for documents to come through. It was a polite request. But in my journal, I voiced my less polite frustration at the government office.

"DAS does not want to give me an identity card, a *cedula*. The whole family got their I.D. cards except me. They are so profoundly disorganized in that office. And no wonder because they keep changing personnel every few months! So, no one knows who we are anymore."

On the home front I was recovering from another bout of cough and fever. This time Andy was ill, too. Matthew stayed in splendid health and so he was appointed chief cook.

"Matthew," I called from my bedroom, "did you manage to make the meatloaf?"

"It's in the oven. I couldn't find oatmeal. I put wheat germ in."

Ah, well.

Becky wrapped up potatoes to bake alongside the meatloaf and Harold sliced a melon before having to run off to meetings. After supper the kids washed dishes without complaint.

I bragged about them in a letter home. "Our kids always pull together during tough situations."

I had learned the Colombian way to wash dishes and preferred it—a sponge rubbed in a tub of soap paste and wiped on dishes under a tap of cool running water. Colombians looked aghast at the North American way of filling a sink with hot water and soapsuds. Why collect the dirt from all the dishes and rub it around on the rest of the dishes?

They felt the same about washing bodies. Bathtubs seemed to horrify our friends. Why sit in your dirt when the point is to wash it away? The Colombian homes we'd seen had only showers, no bathtubs.

My doctor, the *real* doctor this time, had diagnosed secondary bronchitis and impressed on me that I was very sick and should rest and not do anything for a week. On my nightstand were two antibiotics, an inhaler and allergy pills.

The maid was shocked. "Those are so bad for you!" I had to endure many a lecture about home remedies I should be trying instead.

Andrew was home recovering, too, and to ease boredom, I suggested he use the computer to type a letter to his uncle, my brother John and his wife Janice. I ran it off on the printer and he took it to the table where he very precisely drew a box outline around it with ruler and pencil.

I sipped coffee. Noting his precision, I asked him what he wanted to be when he grew up. Without a second's hesitation he said, "A scientist and a missionary." Oh! I couldn't speak for a full half minute. I never expected Andrew to want to be a missionary. He loved the outdoors and his experience here, mostly indoors, had been constricting.

Good Lord, I thought, maybe we're doing something right after all.

Home life was very different from what it had been in small-town Canada where life was relaxed and the kids could leave their bikes out on the front lawn overnight with never a worry of losing them.

We also had learned to be flexible with schedules here, especially mealtime. Meals were prepared whenever other meetings ended. One day I hurried home from a women's meeting. It was 5:30 and I thought Harold and the kids would be waiting for me to make supper.

As I approached our front door, I saw a group of neighbours across the street. They called me over. My neighbour Constanza was on the sidewalk with a group of young men, university students from neighbouring houses.

"*Señora* Doroti, you are a Bible teacher. What is it that you teach?"

They kept asking questions and I loved the challenge to explain in plain language what the Bible taught about Jesus and a personal connection with God. Young adults were my favorite people to converse with as they enjoyed challenging my ideas. I enjoyed myself immensely and decided supper could wait.

When I finally tore myself away, I found Rebecca with the young boys in our back patio trying to teach Mitzi to climb the lemon tree. She was sure her little dog was exceptional and could accomplish anything. Matthew was calling ideas down to them from his bedroom window and Harold was in the office. No one demanded supper. I relaxed then, too, and remembered, *I love that about this country! Time is elastic.*

With the church construction behind us, we could focus on our first furlough, which was fast approaching, just seven weeks away. So much needed to be done. I was writing a skit for our kids to rehearse and perform in churches. We had reports and slide shows to compile with accompanying music. Family songs to rehearse that we'd sing in church services. The kids actually enjoyed those rehearsals, imagining we were the Von Trapp family.

Then there were the purchases to make before the trip.

"I'm making a list of all these gifts we want to buy to bring to our friends and family back home," I said. "Goodness! There must be a hundred things to buy."

"Add to that—I need a better white shirt," Harold said.

"Oh yes! To get up on church platforms every Sunday through three whole months, oh yes. We all need new clothes and decent shoes."

Medellín, fortunately, was a great place to buy clothes, a fabric mecca for clothing companies like Esprit. We could buy classy clothes for much less than back home. I had already bought my favorite khaki slacks, and a khaki and cream pinstriped shirt. I was especially proud of that shirt because of the unusual design. The buttoned lapel ran in a slanted line from the waist on the left to the shoulder on the right. *Haute couture!* I was *not* going to look like a missionary just off the boat.

To complicate things, Harold was caught up in a battle to replace documents. The Saturday before the inauguration of the church, his briefcase had been stolen out of the jeep. All his papers, I.D., license, car ownership, everything. Gone! Plus, he had been to the bank that day to cash a cheque and that money was gone, too.

"There's too much stress," I complained. "I think we're ready for a month of sheer holiday. NOT three months of travelling, reporting and being on show."

"Others have done it," Harold said in a weary voice. "We can too. How did the Apostle Paul do those endless missionary journeys?"

"Ha!" I answered. "He probably welcomed prison to get a rest!"

37   What we got from prison

Soon after the church building was completed, it was time for another baptism service. Four young men had taken the membership classes and asked to be baptized. The congregation was eager to celebrate the baptism in our own church.

However, we had no baptismal tank. What to do?

Harold heard that some missionaries had started chapel services in a Medellín prison and were baptizing inmates by immersion there. This was accomplished with a portable tank they were permitted to bring into the prison. So off he went to investigate.

Yes, he could borrow the tank. It was stored inside the prison,

Chapter 37

Cárcel Bellavista. He would need to retrieve it from there.

He and Galen got permission to enter the prison compound. Through the corridors they went, steel doors clanging shut behind them after each section they passed through. They reached a large common room and heard singing. They were led toward the music and walked into a room converted into a chapel.

Here they saw many inmates seated in rows of chairs, heartily singing hymns and choruses. Harold and Galen were told to wait for the service to end.

"No problem, man," Galen said. "It's just great to see these smiling faces. In spite of being locked up, these guys are actually smiling."

Bellavista means beautiful view but Harold told me later, "There were no windows. No view at all. The rooms were only lit by light bulbs."

After the service the inmates milled around Harold and Galen in curiosity as they retrieved the pieces of plywood, metal rails and the heavy rubber lining that made up the tank. At our church on the Saturday night before the service, Harold and Galen assembled the tank and filled it with water, ready for the next day.

Next morning, we arrived at church.

Oh no! Water on the floor. The tank was leaking badly.

Harold's spirits sank. How would the rubber be repaired? He felt exhausted from the previous weeks of construction, then inauguration, followed by two weeks of outreach campaigns.

"I don't have the emotional energy to give the sermon this morning," he whispered to me. I tried not to look shocked and whispered back, "I'll pray for you. You'll find the strength. It'll come."

I silently prayed as the men cast about for a solution to the leak.

After some time, a special adhesive was found for the rubber. The leak was stopped and the water mopped up. When the service got underway, it seemed that a special grace came over Harold. He delivered an inspirational talk on the topic "Hope." And hope was just what we needed that day. Hope that the adhesive would hold.

In the evening we returned to church for the baptismal service. Had the tank held?

Yes! The leak had been stopped.

Then a new challenge faced us. Two men of our church, Bruno and Jon, had mounted a red spotlight above the tank.

"*Que emoción!*" they enthused. "At the time of the baptism we'll turn all the lights off and just have this red light over the tank."

We took a moment to think how best to respond.

"Well, would we want the church to look like a nightclub or like a sanctuary? We can have the spotlight, yes. How about a white bulb instead of red?" They agreed and ran to the store to buy a white bulb.

What a night! *Que emoción*, indeed. Our first baptismal service in our own church building was an exciting event. The sanctuary was filled—we had to carry up an extra bench from the basement.

Four men were baptized under the white spotlight with Harold dipping each one under the water. The loud applause as each one rose from underwater testified to how all our hearts were touched by their stories. It was not an easy choice for these guys to make a life change in this neighbourhood.

I confess, though, my mind was half on the refreshments since there were about twice as many people as we'd expected. We church women had decided on cheese, bread and juice following the service. But I knew we'd need more than we'd prepared.

Chapter 38

After the service we asked William to dash out to get more bread. Meanwhile, we cut all the cheese pieces in half. Before the service I'd found Freddy busy downstairs shelling passion fruit, maracuyas, and blending the juice with sugar. Now, water and sugar were added, and everyone got only half a cup of this delicious juice. But no one minded. Everyone was thrilled to get anything at all.

As our family trundled off home after cleanup and after draining the tank, the kids' comments summed up our feelings. "Everyone was happy there!"

All the church people had pitched in, creating a close sense of community, welcoming with open arms and hearts the new members. We couldn't ask for more.

 ## 38   The café in Envigado

"It's funny that in this country that produces great coffee, I can't find a coffee shop. Not the kind you can relax in," I said to another ex-pat one day.

"Well, Dorothy, you're always driving around in those poor barrios. Try driving to Envigado where the wealthy live. They have coffee shops the way we have in North America."

"Isn't that Escobar's neighbourhood?"

"So? He's not likely to hang around coffee shops."

One afternoon Harold and I drove to Envigado in search of a café.

We found a delightful one set back from the street and freshly painted in pastel colours. It looked like a postcard from Paris. We parked the jeep and happily took our seats at one of four outdoor tables with cloth napkins and comfortable chairs. We were the only ones on the patio. I ordered lemon pie and Harold ordered apple pie. Just like in Canada. And cappuccinos, of course.

We couldn't stop smiling, revelling in the luxury. After our pie, we leaned back, enjoying the cappuccinos.

A jeep pulled up at the curb with four men inside. A portly man got out from the back seat and walked toward the café. He chose a table, one over from ours, and sat himself down on the far side of his table, facing us. Behind him came three men in suits and ties, each one carrying an Uzi. They took up standing positions in a semicircle behind his chair, crossing their arms and resting their guns on their crossed arms.

Harold and I held our breath. We sat up straight.

"I think we're finished now," we whispered to each other. The bill had already been paid so we got up, tried to look casual, and slowly walked to our car.

Once there, we breathed.

"Oh my! That wasn't Escobar but—"

"His brother, for sure. Looks just like his picture!"

We never went to that café again. But I've never again tasted such a good cappuccino.

39   Harold chases robbers

A few months before we left on furlough, two painters came to repaint the inside walls of the garage. The garage was actually a room in the house with one side completely open to the living room so that when our jeep was parked at home, we saw it from any place we sat in the living room. This is a common building design in Medellín homes. It's economical and also serves as a security measure for the vehicle. We had partially blocked the view of the garage from the living room by installing a tall bookshelf.

The garage itself was not an ugly space. When the jeep was away, the garage became a wonderful playroom for the kids. Its plastered walls and ceiling were painted a cream colour like the rest of the house. The floor was a beautiful caramel-coloured ceramic tile. Even the driveway was paved in ceramic tiles. Colombians kept their garage floors and their driveways as immaculately scrubbed as floors in the rest of the house. We often saw maids outdoors running electric floor polishers over tiled driveways.

The jeep in the garage next to the *sala*.

When the jeep was at home, it was an unavoidable part of the home décor, gas smell and all. This was not a problem, though, because the windows in the house had glass louvers permanently cemented open. Traffic noises became so familiar that I hardly heard them. Cars and trucks sped up or wound down depending whether they were moving up our hill or down. Motorcycles without mufflers roared by. And often there was the rhythmic clip-clop, clip-clop of horse-drawn carts.

When the two painters came to add a new coat of paint, we knew enough by then that to leave a worker unsupervised was a non-Colombian thing to do. Only ignorant foreigners turned their backs on hired help. So, Harold dutifully sat on the living room sofa reading the morning paper while keeping an eye on the painters across the room.

The phone rang.

It was a neighbour, a Colombian living near the bottom of our street.

"Come quick! I live across from the house of your friends who are away on a trip, no *cierto*? Come quick—I think their house is being robbed! Just now I saw three people breaking into the front door. They're in the house right now."

Harold jumped up and rushed to the front door. There he stopped.

"Hey, you two," he called to the painters, "come with me! Thieves are breaking into a neighbour's house."

The two painters, each standing on a chair, stared across the room at each other, wide-eyed.

"Us? No. No, we don't chase robbers. *Que locura*. That's crazy."

"They're getting away! Come on. We have to go right now!"

"*Por favor, señor*, that's dangerous. We could get killed."

One hand on the front door handle Harold stood waving them on. "If you don't come, I'll not pay you. Not one peso!" The painters in their spotted whites looked dolefully at each other like sad-faced circus clowns.

"If you like," added Harold, "you can stay a ways behind me. I'll go ahead and you stand watch." Slowly the painters climbed off their chairs, laid down their brushes and reluctantly followed down the street.

The previous time Harold had promised to watch that same friend's house, there had also been trouble. Then, Harold had mounted a side stairway of that house and surprised two ruffians cutting their way through a wooden door with machetes. They threatened Harold when he confronted them, waving their machetes at him.

But Harold, believing every wrong must be made right, stood his ground. The thieves had suddenly shrugged their shoulders, cursed and run off, seemingly afraid to get entangled with a foreigner.

Now, from a distance, Harold saw that the front door of that house stood open. As he neared the gate, out walked three people, two young men and a woman. They strode confidently down the front walk: all three gave Harold and his painters looks of disdain.

The painters cringed, wrung their hands and whispered, "*Ave Maria!*"

Then, as though they were out for a morning stroll, the thieves sauntered away down the street.

"Hey, we can't just let them get away," Harold shouted. "After them!"

The thieves started to run.

Harold took up the chase. The painters, already having served beyond the call of duty, retreated.

As Harold ran, he called in a loud voice, "*Ladrones! Ayuda!* Robbers! Help!"

He caught up to the thieves and was right on their heels. One of the men stopped, swung around, pointed a knife at Harold, and shouted, "Leave off!"

Then the thief turned and kept running.

Harold took up the chase again, calling out, "Thieves! Thieves!" Neighbours emerged from doorways and some joined in, running behind Harold.

Around the corner they saw the thieves turn into a yard and disappear through the door of a house. Harold stopped outside this house and a small crowd of neighbours gathered. By now someone had called the police, and soon a black and white *Policía* van pulled up. Guns in hand, policemen hurried to the house and shouted to open the door.

When the police came back out of the house, they marched two of the robbers, a man and woman, out to the van.

"We know where the other one is!" called the neighbours, huddled together for safety. "Right out here hiding. See, behind that bush."

Normally, Medellín folk would refuse to help police capture law-breakers for fear of reprisals, but these neighbours must have been caught up in the excitement and trusted in the anonymity of the crowd.

All three thieves were pushed into the back of the van. Then, the police ordered Harold into the front seat. They drove to the nearest police station, a small, red-brick guardhouse with windows on three sides. It stood just three blocks from our house. This is where the van stopped. It was one of the new C.A.I. posts: *Comandos de Atención Inmediata*, Immediate Attention Commandos.

A station of the Commandos Acción Inmediata.

To ensure better police protection, these mini police stations had recently been built all over the city, often at main intersections or next to small playgrounds where they could do double duty and keep playground equipment from being stolen. The usual C.A.I. structure was only as large as a toolshed. There, two policemen with guns stood guard.

Sadly, many policemen were assassinated during our years in Colombia. Just months after this incident, this particular C.A.I. centre was blown up by a bomb and the policemen killed.

Now with the thieves locked in the van, a policeman motioned for Harold to follow him. He led him away from the little building to a shade tree on the boulevard.

"Please reconsider whether you really want to press charges," the policeman said. "You know, *señor*, this is the very band of thieves we've been hunting. It's a pleasure to get rid of them. Nevertheless, I must tell you that what you've done today is a very foolish thing. You've put yourself in danger. If you press charges, they'll only be in jail for two months.

"Today they had knives, but in a few months, they'll come after you with guns. So why should we put them in jail? *No tiene razón.* It doesn't make sense. It would be a favour for everyone if we arranged something. We could load them up, take them up the mountainside and…" Here the officer slowly drew his finger across his throat. "Si?"

Harold blinked hard. Was he hearing correctly? The officer seemed sincere.

In spite of the warning, Harold insisted on filling in the papers to record the incident and press charges. After all, we were Mennonite Brethren missionaries. Pacifists.

But the words of the policeman stuck in our minds. We often wondered how soon the thieves would be freed and what reprisal we should expect. From that day on we drew the front curtains every day as soon as the sun sank behind the mountains. And every time we drove up to our house in the jeep, we looked up and down the street and waited for any strangers to pass on by before rolling aside the garage door that opened into the house.

Then, just months after the day of the chase, while we were in Winnipeg on furlough, an explosion sheared away the front wall of the neighbour's house and blew out our windows.

Our Colombian friends took it more seriously than we did.

"You must definitely move to a different house," they told us. "This is what happens here. There is always a payback. Why do you think no one gets involved in cases like these?"

And they whispered, "What was Harold thinking?"

~~~~~

These scenes rolled through my mind as I lay in bed that Friday night, August 18, 1989, the day we arrived back in Medellin from furlough. The day the assassination of Luis Galán kicked off the major drug wars.

I had checked the kids' beds for glass and was relieved there was none. Not in the beds. The Lego, though, would be a job to clean up. But that was for the morning.

Harold, blessed with the ability to drop off quickly, had fallen asleep.

In the darkness I watched shadows on the wall weaving over the stripes of light cast through the venetian blind. The breeze ruffled the metal slats of the blind. Somewhere down the street a radio played merengue music. People were dancing.

PART III
AUGUST 1989

 ## 40   Peace, peace when there is no peace

Returning to Medellín after furlough, we were eager to see our church community again. The church people had been joyful and energetic before we left them. Some members had strayed in our absence but black sheep or white sheep, they were *our* sheep. My heart felt warm just thinking of them. There wasn't a single one that didn't tackle enormous challenges in their everyday lives. I marvelled at the optimism that kept them sane and active. How did they do it?

On our first Sunday back at church, the sanctuary still felt new after our three months away. I was happy to see our people again, yet could sense a new weight of heaviness. Everyone felt the loss of Luis Galán, assassinated just two days earlier.

Everyone hoped that the President's announcement of "total war" against the drug lords and mafia would not affect our plans, and that we could pursue the dreams we and our church people had envisioned together.

By Tuesday, though, an infuriated Pablo Escobar had already bombed a lot of buildings in Medellín and threatened to bomb many more.

Harold was scheduled to go up to the barrio Doce de Octubre to lead a Bible study in the home of new converts. This barrio, hugging the mountainside across the city from Salvador, was known for its gangs and violence. Taxi drivers refused to drive up there after dark.

Our co-workers, Albert and Anna Enns, had taken over teaching this group but the Ennses were on leave and Harold agreed to fill in. He was eager for me to join him since we had become friends with the host couple.

I felt reluctant to leave the kids alone, given the new level of violence and bombing, but I agreed to go. Like every day near the equator, by six-thirty the sun had dropped behind the mountains and darkness set in. Before leaving, I gave the kids strict instructions.

"Stay inside with the door locked. Obey your brother Matthew. Never open the door for anyone, not even if they say they're the police. If anyone phones do *not* tell them your parents are away."

Then Harold and I trundled off down the hill in our squeaky jeep, praying that the kids would be fine. Our house was not near any important building and I was sure we were not in danger from bombs, especially given that our house had already been targeted.

Each barrio formed its own intricate maze of intertwining streets. There were no main roads running horizontally along the mountain connecting neighbourhoods. We drove all the way down from one and then all the way up to another.

It was drizzling. As the jeep jostled us up and down between the potholes, we watched warily for rocks on the road. It was common practice for thieving gangs to lay a few large rocks to obstruct the road. The thieves waited in hiding nearby until the vehicle stopped and the driver stepped out to remove the rocks. Then they would move in to seize the car and valuables.

But we met no obstacles that night. We arrived at a street that ran tightly alongside a cliff that dropped sharply off the mountainside. Looking down I saw what looked like a ghetto, but what I knew from experience was a working-class neighbourhood: hundreds of houses closely packed facing helter-skelter in all directions, like Lego blocks dropped in a heap. Roofs interlocked in a crazy-quilt pattern. There wasn't a street that ran straight for more than a block before sharply turning. From our vantage point above, it looked as though in the jumble below there were no visible streets.

Suddenly Harold braked the jeep and turned toward the cliff side.

"What are you *doing*!" I shouted, "There's no road here!"

He treated my remark man-style. Silence.

I gripped the bar on the dash and peered into the darkness. The jeep bumped over the curb and down a narrow dirt bank, then dropped past the roofline of a house. It landed with a thump on a tiny patch of concrete that was, wonderfully, horizontal.

"This is the only way to get here?" I asked.

"Much faster than the regular road. One member of the study group lives in this house and lets us park here."

Before the engine died down, four young boys appeared out of the darkness and surrounded our jeep. Harold jumped down and they crowded around him.

"*Hola, Padre! Que tal, Padre?* What's up, Father?" they called out.

I smiled. They thought Harold was a priest. I looked down at the bright red pantsuit I wore. I could hardly pass for any religious order.

Their little faces beamed up at us and they asked me, "Are you going to the meeting?"

"*Si, si, a la reunión,*" I answered. "*Y ustedes?*"

"No, no. We guard *el auto. Tranquilo. Relax.* We guard it well."

We thanked them and walked down the hill toward the hosting couple's house. When we returned, Harold would hand out *pesos* to the boys.

"They're so happy to see you," I said.

"Oh, yes. Do a good job, too. Without them, every visit we'd lose a headlight or a side mirror. Or worse."

We reached a well-painted house with a tiny porch, very different from houses in the neighbourhood of the church. A sturdily built man of about fifty unlocked and opened the solid wooden door. His wife, with a happy head of curls, greeted us with kisses on the cheek. *Bienvenidos!*

Although advanced in age, they were childlike in spiritual matters. On a previous visit after Harold and I had taught the lesson, the woman had looked at me and said, "Oh, so that's how it's done? You read the Bible and you pray to God. That's how you live like a Christian?"

I had assured her it was a good place to start.

Seated around their *sala* now were three men and six women. As was the custom, we walked around to shake hands with each of them. Our host insisted we take the only two armchairs in the room. The foreigner must be honoured. It was embarrassing. This was always the case in every home we visited, even when there was only a bed or cot to sit on.

The study topic that evening was peace. "Peace I leave with you; my peace I give to you," Jesus had said. "Not as the world gives…"

In subdued voices the group tried to build a picture of peace. What would peace look like? They offered suggestions of what it could look like. Safe streets. Calm nights. Less tension during the days.

But talk of peace didn't last.

During the coffee time, talk quickly moved to the new civil war. Several of the group were managers of small businesses, their livelihoods now tenuous.

"When will this war be over?" they asked each other, "When will Medellín be normal?"

"Aren't you foreigners nervous?" they asked us. "Why aren't you leaving? Don't you know that a lot of people are leaving Medellín?"

We assured them we felt at peace because we were confident that we were just where we were meant to be.

As we kissed them each goodnight and walked back up to our jeep perched on the hilltop, we all assumed Harold would be back the next week and the week after that, for many weeks. These were people under our care and we planned to work with them for years to come.

Back at the jeep I saw three boys sitting on the wide front bumper. They were laughing up at a youngster admiring his reflection in a side mirror. I loved to see them laughing, enjoying these hours together, forgetting the oppressions of the times. After handing coins into eager little hands, Harold steered the jeep toward home.

Arriving at our driveway, I carefully looked up and down the street. In the light of the street lamps, the street and sidewalks looked deserted. I jumped down, turned the key, and pushed with all my might on the heavy garage door, sliding it to the side as quickly as I could. Then Harold scooted the jeep inside. I pushed hard to roll the door closed. The lock snapped shut.

I sighed and looked around. Home free. Kids in bed. All well. Peace for the moment.

41   Croissants, soccer and bombs

Sunday, August 27. It was the end of our first full week back in Medellín after our furlough. We were together as a family, driving home from the morning church service. We had invited a group of young people to the house that afternoon to watch a soccer game on television.

"Let's stop at a bakery and pick up fresh croissants," I said.

Harold parked the jeep on a slanting pavement on San Juan Avenue and ran across the street to the bakery.

Immediately, two soldiers in combat uniform with rifles flanked the jeep. They peered in from both sides through the open windows to look at me in the front seat and our four kids in the back.

"*Señora*," they asked, "what do you want here?" Only then did I notice we had stopped in front of a bank, the *Banco Cafetero*. Our bumper was just a metre from the front door, practically touching the front windows. Several branches of this bank had been bombed during the week and I realized these soldiers were on guard to prevent anyone parking a car bomb near it.

They seemed so young to me, mere boys. I felt sorry for them. What a tiresome job–dangerous but at the same time very dull. All day they guarded a two-metre strip of concrete.

"Will you *demora?*"

"No, no," I assured them with a smile, "we won't be here anytime at all. We're buying croissants, *no mas*." They smiled back, but stood pasted to our jeep. While waiting for Harold's return, they entertained themselves by leaning their heads into the windows and staring at the kids' blonde hair.

I liked it that they kept smiling and joking, yet the whole time we waited there, my mind was busy silently pleading, *Don't explode now, bank, while we're here. Please.*

That afternoon Harold and Matthew carried the television down from upstairs and set it up in our *sala*. We had a Sony TV with rabbit ears antenna we had bought in a basement mall in Medellín. In 1989 there were only three TV channels available in Medellín. One channel came on the air daily at 8:30 a.m., another at 11:00 a.m. and the third channel only started programming at 6:00 p.m. But the soccer game was important and would be telecast during the afternoon.

The group of young people from church arrived, eager to watch their Colombian soccer team play against Paraguay in a World Cup qualifier. I enjoyed hearing their animated debate over the strength of individual players. Spanish is such beautiful, musical language. They sat with our kids and Harold, all soon engrossed in the soccer game on TV.

Then BOOM! About four o'clock in the afternoon the noise of an explosion shook the house.

"Another bomb," one of the youth laconically commented, without taking his eyes off the game.

"The mafia say they have thousands of bombs ready to destroy whatever they want to destroy," another stated without looking away from the TV screen.

"That one was close," Harold commented, "probably on the San Juan."

Two of the guys stood up to look out the front window but not seeing anything new, they focused again on the game. For the moment, the game caused more tension. Though Colombia eventually qualified for the World Cup, that particular game ended sadly. Paraguay 2, Colombia 1.

When the game ended Harold said, "Let's go see where the bomb hit." They eagerly piled into the jeep, ready for a distraction, while I went to the kitchen to make ham and cheese croissants and hot chocolate.

Always room for one more. Harold packs youth into our jeep.

There was no door between the small kitchen and the back patio, merely a gate of metal bars that slid to the side when opened. Nothing kept out the wind or rain or small creatures. A cool breeze was blowing in now making it a pleasant prospect to think of a drink like hot chocolate. I barely had time to set out the lunch before the jeep returned.

"That was close to us all right," the youth exclaimed excitedly. "It destroyed the bank on the San Juan!"

"Not the one we stopped next to this morning?" I asked Harold in alarm.

"About a block from there. The one where we always go to deposit our rent money."

"Then how will we pay the rent this week? It's the end of the month."

"I don't know. The landlord will have to figure that one out."

After the snack, the youth thanked me, some with the usual kiss on the cheek and others a handshake, and then left for their homes.

That evening an important membership meeting was planned at the church. I thought I should attend. But the next day was the first day of a new school year for the kids so I wanted them to get to bed at a good hour. Especially Conrad who would be starting first grade.

Matthew was a capable babysitter. I gave them the usual instructions, "Keep the front room lights on. Don't open the door for anyone, not even a policeman in uniform."

Then we kissed them goodnight.

I felt good about the security of the house. All the windows had metal bars. The front door and garage doors were built of steel in wide bars, covered with tempered bubble glass to soften what might otherwise have the look of a prison. Surrounding the back courtyard was a concrete block wall eight feet high, bordered on three sides by neighbours' courtyards.

The streets were clothed in dusk as the jeep bumped its way across the city towards the barrio of Salvador. We dodged potholes and pedestrians, zigzagging our way first down the hill from our home and then up the far mountainside. Between closely packed rows of wooden doors and wooden shutters battered with age, we pushed along sometimes feeling we were close enough to reach out and touch the old men in ragged ponchos with three days growth of beard squatted on concrete stoops.

Although the late afternoon wind had picked up, the weather was warm. Young lovers, arms locking, lounged in doorways that opened directly from homes onto the narrow streets. Here and there between the houses were open cafes with two or three tables huddled together. On rough wooden stools men of varying ages, shirts unbuttoned, bent forward in conversation, gesturing to companions over a collection of empty beer bottles.

Our jeep climbed one steep street after another, turning one sharp corner after another before stopping in front of the church. I looked at this new building with pleasure. What a happy change from the bare concrete pad that had sat there before.

Across the narrow street stood a tight row of houses of assorted colours and window openings. Little balconies were stuck on here and there from which the locals got entertainment watching local boys remove our jeep's hubcaps or side mirrors on warm Sunday evenings. It seemed they thought that if we foreigners were *tonto* enough to park our jeep on their street in the dark, why should they not help themselves?

That Sunday evening a good number of the faithful made it out to the evening service. There was dear little Silvia with her children. There was Marina, a fifteen-year-old trying to build a new way of life. Her family disowned her when she rejected the prostitution practised in her home. Jaime led a few choruses strumming guitar. He dreamt of university and escaping the *barrio* but his mind had been short-circuited from years of taking *bazooka*, crack, the poor man's cocaine.

Dory and her husband Francisco were seated ahead of me each at one end of a bench with a spate of children between them, all orderly, singing with enthusiasm.

Someone stood to pray and I got an attack of the giggles. This is most inappropriate but had happened to me a number of times at the most solemn of moments. The reason for this was a funny incident that happened in the church when we were brand new to Medellín.

Colombian pastors from various regions at our table.

The church had hosted a conference of pastors from other regions. Harold and I sat in a pew about half way from the front. The guest speaker was preaching from behind the pulpit and it would be Harold's job to thank the speaker once he finished. We were new in the language, so Harold, not wanting to miss his cue, sat on the edge of our pew. I leaned over to make a comment to him. And just at that moment the speaker ended his talk with a question that sounded to us like, "Who enjoyed the message we just heard?"

Caught off guard and thinking it was his turn to speak, Harold stood up and looked around, smiling at the assembly. Everyone looked at him, grinned brightly and covered their mouths to keep from laughing out loud.

Elizabeth from Cali later explained, "The speaker *did* start to ask who had enjoyed the message but then twisted the sentence into a joke and asked who had fallen asleep during his talk!"

And Harold had popped up and smiled so innocently!

Every time I remembered that embarrassing moment that had happened on these very benches, I got the giggles.

That Sunday night the important church business was eventually settled. We said goodnight to the members, hugging and kissing all the *hermanos* and *hermanas* in the Colombian custom.

One angular woman, Sofie, pulled me aside, "Hermana," she said, "I want you to know that I'm so sorry for you and I have started to pray every day that God will protect your children and keep them safe."

"Thank you, dear sister. That means a lot to me." We hugged goodbye.

On the drive home I said to Harold, "That was so kind of Sofie to tell me that, and yet it actually increases my anxiety. The Colombians in this barrio are so used to violence. The situation must be more serious than I realize if *they* think we're in danger."

After the half-hour drive bumping through potholed roads in the dark, we pulled up to our short driveway. I let out a sigh of relief to see the house looking untouched, the doors shut tight, light on in the front room.

Inside, the only sound was the faint music of Tchaikovsky's violin concerto coming from the cassette player upstairs in the young boys' room. Every night Conrad insisted on this same piece of music, no other, to lull him to sleep. It was near the end of the piece so the boys must be asleep already.

I breathed a sigh of relief. Conrad would be ready for his first day of school tomorrow.

We found Matthew reading and Becky tucking Mitzi into her doggie bed. All safe at home. Sofie's prayer was working.

 ## 42 Bring on that great Colombian coffee

Monday, August 28. We woke at six to the raucous call of the newspaper vendor striding up the street like some peddler in a Dickens novel.

"El Colombiano-o-o, El Colombiano-o-o!"

Harold pulled on pants and rushed outside to buy a paper. I slipped into my purple gingham housecoat and took the slippery tile stairs carefully, my mind in a Monday morning fog.

Harold settled on the sofa to go through the paper.

"What's the news?" I asked. "What's been happening?"

"Nine banks bombed yesterday," he announced from behind the paper.

"Really?! Nine banks bombed here in Medellín?"

"Yeah, and this is the day I need to go pay bills at our bank."

"The rent bill, though, we can't pay. That bank is gone, right? Boy, I hope that at least the bank where we have our own accounts is still there. Hey, can you help me get the kids moving? First school day today and I'm not used to these lunch boxes. We're a little behind."

It was a warm, sunny morning so I decided breakfast would be cold cereal and milk. There were only a few cold cereals available in

Medellín stores: Corn Flakes, frosted or plain; and Rice Krispies in three flavours: plain, strawberry or chocolate.

Milk was not processed for long life. It was sold in plastic bags and went sour after two days. Fortunately, Matthew was up and dressed. I sent him down the street to buy milk at the corner shop.

While the children ate their cereal Harold read aloud a family-friendly devotional story. Then we prayed together. We had a long list to pray for. We asked God to bless our families back home, our team in Colombia, the missionaries in other countries, and our church people. Then we prayed for our children and their teachers as they launched into this new school year. We knew our families back home in Canada prayed earnestly for our safety. We ourselves rarely thought to pray for safety. That would be like praying to have enough air to breathe that day.

By seven-thirty the kids, their faces scrubbed, wearing new clothes and loaded with new notebooks were assembled on the step outside the front door eager to board the bus. Conrad was thrilled to start school. He stood proudly with his backpack and lunch box. We took a picture of this historic day, never dreaming he'd have a "first day at school" very soon again.

A loud honk announced the arrival of the white and red *buseta*, a small twelve-passenger hired bus. I felt a slight knot in my stomach about sending them off through the city where nine bombs had exploded the day before. But the Colombian driver was experienced. He would know where to drive to avoid trouble. But now I did think to pray. *Lord, please send your angels to guard the children.*

After a second cup of coffee, Harold picked up the keys.

"Paying bills at the bank," he announced.

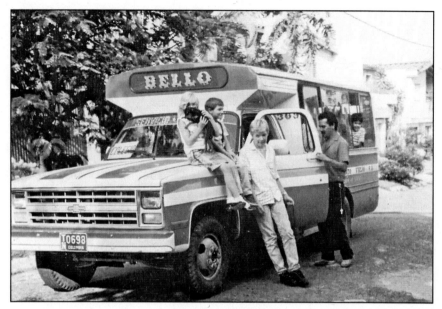

The school buseta.

We stood in the doorway and hugged. Normally leaving on errands called for a peck on the cheek and "See you later." But today we hugged. I planted my face into his shoulder and said, "Now be careful, okay?"

Silly thing ever to say to Harold. Careful was for sissies.

"Uh-huh," he answered for my sake. Then he climbed into the jeep and trundled off down the hill. I found myself sending up a silent prayer again. *Please Lord, don't let our bank explode when he is in it.*

He was back safely at one o'clock. I felt relieved.

Then, the phone rang. It was our boss, Harold Ens, calling from the Mission office in Kansas. I could picture him, his tall, gangly frame perched on a swivel chair, his hand pushing up his glasses.

"We're concerned here," he said. "The Canadian office called me because they're upset about an article that came out on the front page of *The Winnipeg Free Press*. It's got a family photo of you and the kids.

It tells about the bomb that damaged your house and so on. Did you give a phone interview to the reporter?"

"Yes, we did. On Friday. The reporter is an old friend from way back, Lorna Dueck. You don't think it was a good thing to do?"

"Well, the office personnel here feel it could endanger you in some way. Do you think so?"

"We don't feel that way. Right now there's a lot of anti-American feeling but being Canadian, we still feel safe."

"Well, we want you to take every precaution. This morning the Canadian Broadcasting Corporation phoned to get your number but I refused to give it to them. They wanted to interview you over radio. Some show called *As It Happens*, I think."

Darn it! I thought, I would have loved to talk with the CBC.

"Another thing," he went on, "we want you to know that the office is giving you the freedom to decide how much of this you can take. If any family there wants to get out and go to Cali or Bogotá for a while, they should feel free to do so. The travel bill would be covered."

We immediately called our Medellín team members to discuss what people were now calling The Situation. We were soon gathered in our living room: Galen and Linda Wiest, Peter and Eva Loewen, Harold and myself. Albert and Anna Enns were away on furlough.

I got ready to serve coffee.

"The home office says we're free to make our own decisions and get out of the city for a while if we want to," we reported. "Go to Cali or Bogotá."

Each one voiced an opinion.

"Travel? I wouldn't want to be a foreigner on the highway now. You get stopped at the guerrilla checkpoints and you're soon on your way to visit Mr. Pablo Escobar wherever *he's* living. Doesn't sound like a good—"

"Yeah, if the city's any indication of what's out on the highways—just now when we were out at noon, we passed through four separate police roadblocks, and that was just on a ten-minute drive to the grocery store."

"It would be terrible to have to travel now."

"Let's not get all worried. No one's interested in us so far. Next Tuesday is the deadline that Escobar gave the government to decide if they'll approve extradition to the States. He's really mad at the Americans."

"Let's just lay low, wait it out, see if there's more action."

"Keep extra cash on hand for emergency. You never know, eh?"

"Yeah, some other groups are saying we should all have our passports up-to-date just in case we have to leave."

"People get all uptight," Harold said. "This could blow over."

Our team disbursed and we waited for the kids to come home.

At 4 p.m. they were dropped off and burst into the house full of excitement. They all talked at once of new classmates and teachers. Little Conrad was green with nausea from the diesel fumes of the bus ride.

"Think you'll like first grade, Conrad?"

"Oh yeah, it's fun. We played war at noon."

Oh brother!

"Now," I said, "you had cereal this morning, but how would you like a bowl of Corn Pops for a snack?"

"Corn Pops! What!? Where did you get them?"

"In the store. I found them today. They've got them here now. And they're made in Colombia, too, so we can always buy them!"

For the next twenty minutes no one raised any topic except

how delicious it was to enjoy the crunchy taste of Corn Pops in a bowl of milk. Then each child sought out their own entertainment. I overheard Andy and Conrad talking about the play gunfights they had had the night before with Matt and Becky while Harold and I were away at the church meeting.

So much for parents' pacifist teaching.

That night I lay in bed thinking about the phone call from the Mission office.

Would we ever consider leaving Medellín? We didn't *want* to leave so what could make us go? We felt adjusted now to Medellín and to Colombian life. We knew the church people, had come to really care for them and feel concern for their welfare. We couldn't abandon them.

A stiff breeze blew in through the louvered windowpanes. The old-fashioned venetian blind slapped up against the window frame rhythmically with a metallic thud. The permanently open windows let in every small noise from the street and from the neighbours' yards. Somewhere a dog barked and then another, until several formed a syncopated serenade.

I heard the whistle of the night watchman. It was faint so I knew he was on the far side of the block. He was a middle-aged man with a weathered face. Mounted on a bicycle he circled the block with a wooden club dangling around his left leg, an ancient pistol in its holster tied to his right side. On cool nights he was covered in a beige *ruana* that hung to his knees turning him into a pale pyramid of a ghost gliding down the hill.

All night he rode round and round the few blocks that were his trust, every half block blowing hard on a whistle hung about his neck. We never understood the purpose of blowing the whistle. Was it an

"All's well" for those lying sleepless on their beds? Was it *"Here I come so please don't show yourself"* for would-be robbers partway through their thievery? Or was it simply a way to keep himself awake through the lonely night?

From the house behind ours, I heard teenagers singing along to American rock music on the radio, *"You are the one for me..."* I smiled with pleasure to hear their accented English.

In the yard next to ours, I could hear the clink of a spoon stirring sugar in a coffee cup on the other side of the wall that separated our backyards. The little Napoleon must be on his back patio enjoying a late night *tinto*. Did he have his gun at his side there, too?

43   Getting nervous

Tuesday, August 29. I woke the next morning to the venetian blind flapping gently in the breeze. It was the twelfth day since our return from furlough. Harold was his usual cheerful morning self, lacing his brown shoes while seated on the bed making the mattress bounce.

"So, what's for breakfast today?" he asked. "Corn Pops?"

"Nu-uh," I managed. "Colombian today. Hot chocolate and buns."

Before seven-thirty, before the kids had gone, the phone rang.

It was our co-worker Peter Loewen.

"So, what's the latest you've heard on The Situation?" Every call these days was about The Situation.

"You got time to get together this morning?" Peter asked. "I feel we should put our heads together on this."

"Sure," Harold answered. "Why don't we meet here? I'll call Galen and Linda. Eight-thirty's okay?"

We three couples held another team meeting. All of us had heard bombs exploding during the night and there was animated speculation as to where and how close to us each bomb had been.

Most of the discussion was centred on The War. Overnight, The War had replaced The Situation.

"What we need to consider and talk about here," Peter said, "is the threat that's been made to kidnap or kill North Americans in protest of the extradition of drug dealers. Some missions are taking it seriously. The Wesleyans and the Covenants are meeting today to make plans. Probably leaving."

"What about the Canadian Baptists?"

"I think they're holding back. Like us. Waiting to see what happens."

"Because if they leave then we'd be in trouble," I said. "The Wiests and us wouldn't have a school for our kids anymore and maybe we'd have to leave, too."

"That's too drastic," Harold cut in. "Things are tense but there's no personal danger yet."

"Our parents called last night," put in Linda. "Everyone back home is nervous. They keep asking why we don't leave. And people are badgering the Mission offices back home asking why they don't take us out of here."

"In some ways it's as safe as it's ever been," said Galen. "The bad guys have files on all of us. How many stories have we heard of kidnapped foreigners being shown a file on all their movements and personal information? If they want us, they've got our addresses and phones. They can come and get us."

"Okay, but one missionary gets kidnapped or killed and the pressure on the offices back home will be huge."

"Yeah. There'd be a big outcry by all the mission agencies for all of us to leave. And fast."

Then everyone jumped in at the same time—

"Not by land, no way."

"Not with guerrillas dressed in military uniforms and stopping cars at fake checkpoints."

"They'd pick us out as foreigners right away and we'd have had it."

"All our blonde kids…"

"You think the guerrillas are working with the drug guys?"

"Why, of course!" said Peter who'd worked for decades in Colombia. "Where do you think the guerrilla armies get the money for their arms and training and all that? No, that's obvious. And where do you think the drug dealers get the bombs and arms and stuff for this drug war? Through their guerrilla connections."

"The news says guerrillas have control of the highways right now. At least around Medellín."

"If land travel is out, that leaves air travel."

"That'll be expensive. And there's always the chance we'd want to leave quickly. We should have extra cash on hand."

"Every family should have a couple hundred American dollars in the house," said Peter. "Dollars are always welcome in any situation."

"Right," His wife Eva said. She had been sitting quietly, hand-quilting a burgundy chair cover. How incongruous, I thought. Such a domestic occupation in our meeting about The War. Now she wondered out loud without raising her eyes from her work, "And what happens if the *mafiosos* and narcos do take over the city?"

"Didn't they long ago?" asked Galen.

We all laughed.

"Okay, say they would take over. The airport's almost an hour out of town. Would that be a problem?"

"No more than it always has been," I put in, thinking of the guerrilla hold-ups on the road to the airport.

Smiles all around.

"But yes," I quickly added, "the military did take control of the airport road the day Galan was shot—"

"It could go the other way quickly."

"Well, that's the other thing," Peter said. "We should be prepared in case it isn't possible to move around as freely as we'd like. It would be wise for every home to have a supply of food stocks just in case it gets ugly for a while and we need to sit it out."

"Good idea." We all nodded, relieved to hear of some concrete action we could take. "Stock up on non-perishables, beans and rice. If we don't need them, they'll last a long time."

"And talking about food," I said, "how about some coffee?"

"Boy, could I use a coffee!" sighed Galen.

I followed the conversation from the kitchen while preparing some the coffee and setting out baking on a platter.

At suppertime that day we talked to the children about The War.

"Now you know, with this war going on, it's especially unsafe for foreigners. From now on you can't go outside at all except to school and church. It's safer that way."

The kids showed little disappointment. They hadn't played outdoors much anyway. There were rare games with the neighbour kids and bicycle rides, but these had always been restricted to the street in front of the house.

At first it had been difficult to adjust. In Manitoba, the front of our home had faced the open prairie. The backyard joined grassy meadows bordered by a winding stream alongside Morden's beautiful golf course. In my experience, playing outdoors was what made kids healthy, vigorous and stable.

Though I fussed inwardly over the loss of play area, the kids seemed to have forgotten their former meadows and were content to build Lego creations or play games by the hour and the day, shut in the house. Or they climbed the lemon tree, sprayed each other with the garden hose, played in the sandbox Harold had made and fed lettuce to the pet rabbits we kept in a cage.

It didn't seem the kids were worried about that new phrase, *The War*. It was starting to worry me, though.

That evening, after the others were tucked in bed, I felt a strong need to communicate with my family in Canada. I wanted to know what they were feeling. But a phone call did not appeal to me. The lines were so poor that words were delayed in transmission, making phone calls awkward.

A relative had once asked during a call, "Dorothy, do you speak English in your home?" She thought the delay in the lines meant I couldn't find the right words to speak. Besides the transmission annoyance, phone calls to North America were expensive. It cost $75 Canadian to make a decent call to Canada.

So instead of calling, I sat down to write a letter at the dining room table. It was almost suppertime but I could relax because I had chicken, potatoes and carrots roasting in the oven. But I didn't relax, even with the carry-me-home-to the-prairie aroma filling the house.

The letter did not flow. It turned out strangely disjointed. Maybe that was due to hearing on the news that six bombs had exploded in Medellín that day.

"Dearest Mom and Dad,

We are all well and content in spite of circumstances. You have no doubt heard much news. We still go to the bank and get our mail and do our work. The kids started school yesterday and there's a good bus driver. We have a good team unity here with the other missionaries. It's great.

"Becky is busy sewing doll clothes and bean bags on the machine. She's very good already. Just makes things up. Andrew is so happy to be back here. He prayed the other night, 'Thank you that we can live in Colombia and thank you that we could have the church people for supper.'

"The kids are strictly inside these days and they understand and don't mind. Conrad is proud to be at school finally and gets home very tired. Matthew is happy to play piano for hours. He often babysits the others for which we are really thankful.

"Don't worry about us. We trust you can experience Jesus' words with us 'My peace I leave with you, not as the world gives'. We love you very much!"

44   Enough to curl my hair

Wednesday, August 30. I woke drowsily. Bombs exploding through the night had broken into my dreams, startling me over and over to half-wakefulness.

"Things are getting worse," I muttered to Harold.

After seeing the kids off to school, I kept an appointment with the hairdresser. After three months of travel my hair needed attention. And maybe something as mundane as a hair appointment might help me forget the stress of The War.

Not to be.

I walked to the hairdressing shop, just a few blocks from our home. Like many salons in Medellín, this one was in the garage of a house. The garage door stood open all day long and opened directly onto the sidewalk. That meant women had their hair dyed, curled or washed all in full view of passersby. Women also had pedicures done close enough to the sidewalk to reach out and touch people. Colombians seemed completely at ease with such lack of privacy.

When I walked in and took my seat, the stylist was engrossed in sharing the latest war news with the several other women in the shop.

I sighed.

"Last night," exclaimed the stylist who lived upstairs, "two little shops right on this road were bombed! Did you see them on your way here?"

"Little shops. That's nothing," scoffed a woman.

"That's right," returned another. "Do you know what they found by the liquor factory last night? Missiles! All set to go off. *Dios mío!* A real war with missiles!"

"Thank God the soldiers found them before they went off."

"We should worry about the economy," said a short woman getting her hair dyed with henna. "Banks are getting blown up, shops and factories too. What will happen to us?"

"Will we still be able to buy food for our families? No, no. I can't imagine…."

"The airport is full of people. All leaving. To another city, another country, who knows?"

"Today they start with the *toque de queda*."

Till now they had talked among themselves and I hadn't said a word. I was sick of war talk. I dreaded getting into a topic that taxed my emotional energy. I was happy they were ignoring me.

Now they turned to me.

"*Señora*," one of them asked, "do you know what the toque de queda is?"

Scissors paused in mid-air.

Five pairs of dark eyes questioned me.

I knew each of those three words but had never heard them in combination. *Toque* was 'touch' and *queda* meant 'to stay'.

I was sick and tired of being an ignorant foreigner. I didn't want explanations. I wanted anonymity. To be left alone.

So, I nodded, *yes*.

They went back to chattering amongst themselves.

"It's ten o'clock, no?" the stylist continued. "And after that if you are out on the street, *bang*, they shoot you, no problem."

Ah, I realized, t*oque de queda*. Curfew.

But I stayed silent.

I knew I was not following the Colombian social rules. In the company of others, one must contribute to the conversation. One must elaborate on one's experience, making it a story. One has an obligation to infuse the group with spirit, create drama. How the Colombians love drama!

I liked these women. They faced the mafia, the guerrillas, the corrupt police force, their changeable government, and they fought back. They fought back with any means at their hands. This morning it was henna and nail polish.

They saw that missiles and bombs were blowing up around them and they said, Fine— let's get our nails done.

Life goes on. That was the great message of the Colombian people to the world. We've been trampled and misused and misguided but we do not despair.

Two days earlier a car bomb had blown up an office building. Before my hair appointment that morning Harold and I had driven by to see the site out of curiosity. There had been nothing to see. The wreckage was gone. All cleaned up and just a space now on the street between buildings, like a tooth missing in the mouth of a six-year-old. We were amazed. Colombians were determined to bounce back.

I felt sad for them. This was *their* salon, *their* city, *their* shops getting blown up. I was an outsider, a stranger with a homeland I could run to. They were stuck in this city with its violent past, violent present and what looked like a violent future.

"That's pretty short," Harold said about my hair when I got home.

"Well, the stylist's mind was on other things. The women said there are missiles around the outskirts of the city. Can that be true?"

"Newspapers talked about that."

That afternoon we walked to our neighbourhood *tienda*, a tiny shop, just a barred window through which we passed our *pesos* to an outstretched hand. Then milk, bread and sugar were passed to us through the bars. On our way home, we happened to meet another foreign couple who lived in the next neighbourhood. We stopped on the street and chatted in English.

"So, what is *your* group deciding?" we asked.

"We're all packing up. Going to Ecuador to wait it out there. Or maybe Cartagena."

"Cartagena! Hey," we laughed, "we'll join you on the beach. Actually, our group is so small, just three families you know. The home office is leaving it up to us as to when or even *if* we leave. We've been meeting day to day to talk it over."

Suddenly, above us, a voice broke into our talk. A *señora* poked her head through a second-floor window and called down to us.

"What are you doing?" she demanded. "Talking English in the street—do you want to tell the whole world where you are so they can come after you?"

Abashed, we whispered goodbye and good luck and parted. We never saw that couple again.

That evening, together with the children, we huddled to watch the Colombian news on our small television. Cameras showed a very congested airport in the capital city of Bogotá. Besides Colombian families fleeing the country, there were rows of American students who had come to Colombia for university studies. Lined up with their baggage, they too were fleeing. Some students were crying. They didn't want to leave.

It was announced that the United States embassy was clearing out all non-essential personnel.

"Evacuating from Bogotá? But nothing much is happening in Bogotá," Harold commented. "Bombings are all here in Medellín."

"The embassy must be expecting major reprisals against Americans."

Tears filled my eyes as I watched. What was happening to this beautiful country? Bogotá was called the Athens of Colombia, and some even called it the Athens of South America, a cultural centre with lots of universities. Yet even from there people were fleeing in fright.

That night a miracle happened in Medellín—complete silence. The *toque de queda* took effect.

No people crowded the sidewalks, no buses rattled through the streets, no cars honked. The myriad vendors and beggars disappeared. Even the watchman with his bicycle bell stayed home. A heavy waiting fell over the city.

Three million silent people.

Just before ten o'clock, curfew time, I heard gunshots.

I ran upstairs, through the gray light of the boys' bedroom where they slept in their bunk beds. As quietly as I could, I slipped the bolt on the steel door and stepped onto the little balcony that faced the street.

But I could see nothing.

Who had fired? At whom and why? Had someone broken curfew in the next street? No commotion followed, only that eerie silence again. No answers.

It came to me how Karen Blixen had written in *Out of Africa* that a single shot in the night felt strangely as though someone had cried out a message in a single word and would not repeat it.

I stood in the silence, straining against the metal railing. It was so silent that for the first time in our two years there, I heard the church bells from the neighbouring barrio ringing on the hour at ten o'clock. Were they calling in vain for the faithful to come to late mass? Or maybe they wanted to say, *Fear not – all shall be well.*

 ## 45   We're not leaving

Thursday morning, August 31. By six-thirty on Thursday morning I heard Matthew whistling in his bedroom, getting ready for school. After the silence of the first night of curfew, every sound seemed sharper and more startling. Our other three kids had recently been after Matthew to teach them to whistle, so whistling was *la mode*, with the off-tune lispings of the younger ones filling the house.

Matthew at the piano early morning.

Matthew was soon at the piano playing a sonata. I worried that the noise would annoy the neighbours. But Harold said, "Between the shouting of the newspaper guy and the papaya vendor, no one's still sleeping."

It was the children's fourth day of the new school year. In the morning they waved goodbye and boarded the school *buseta* as usual. As the bus carried my dear ones away around the corner, I had a moment of panic. What if something *did* happen to them today?

But back inside I was quickly absorbed in preparing for a birthday we would celebrate in our *sala* that morning for our team member, Eva Loewen. I had baked an angel food cake from a mix brought from Canada.

Yet even with cake and coffee in hand, it was a very unbirthday-like atmosphere. Our little group of three couples fell immediately into discussing The War.

"Yesterday three more judges resigned here in Medellín. I can understand that. The drug traffickers vowed to kill ten judges for every Colombian extradited to the U.S."

"Yeah, so far I think 108 judges have resigned since the day the war started, August 18. What's that? Ten, no twelve days ago?"

"Thirteen."

"Did you see the news? How police have free rein now to pick up suspected drug dealers?"

"I read they've detained more than 11,000 people so far. According to the Ministry of Defense."

"Man, it's a nationwide sweep. Do you think they'll finally actually rid the country of drug traffickers?"

"Well, it's a war, eh? Things will get worse, I imagine, before better.

And—"

"Then what are our chances of leaving if things get worse?"

"The airport's pretty isolated. It won't be a target though, will it? How would we—"

"We'd have to fly regardless. Travel by road is totally unsafe. Can't you just see how guerrilla groups will take advantage of all this disorder in the country? Stopping, robbing whoever they like."

"Talking of planes, I heard the army's seized three hundred and forty-six airplanes belonging to traffickers," said Peter. "And more than four hundred ranches, estates and buildings have been taken, too"

"That will *not* improve Escobar's mood," said Galen.

"He's mad about the extraditions to the States, so clearly he has it in for Americans. Galen and Linda, you folks should probably get out before Tuesday," Peter said. "That's September 5, the date scheduled for the extradition. Things will get ugly for Americans. So many threats have been made. And you've got the three little kids."

Peter and Eva were Canadians like our family. Galen and Linda with their three children were Americans.

"When do you think we should leave?"

"This weekend. How about Saturday?"

"Two days to pack?" Galen looked at Linda.

"Well," she answered, "we're just taking our clothes, right? I mean, it's probably just for a couple of weeks."

We all looked at each other and shrugged. We wished we could answer but no one knew.

"What about the rest of us? Are there any precautions we should take?"

"We called the Canadian Embassy. They're not ready for any radical moves yet. They suggest we lie low."

"I agree. Lie low. The time could come when we wouldn't want our presence known here."

"We should be ready to hole up for a while."

"That's right. Be prepared to hole up. At the same time ready to get out on short notice."

"Remember to get that supply of American dollars," Peter mentioned. "And extra food. Non-perishable stuff, you know."

That afternoon, Harold and I went separate ways into town, he to the bank and I to the grocery store. He would get a stash of American dollars and I would buy the non-perishable food. As the taxi wove its way to the Exito supermarket, I tried to decide how much rice and dry beans would be enough. It felt foolish to buy for an unknown future. Surely this would all pass. The uncertainty made my shoulders stiff.

At Exito I piled the cart with five bags of rice and five bags of dried beans. What a clandestine activity. Beans and rice had never been so exciting!

Back home I found I'd had more luck than Harold.

"Too many people had the same idea. Now there are no American dollars to be had in Medellín."

I stowed the bags of rice and brown beans in the pantry.

"Guess we're not the only ones preparing for an emergency," I said, "Are people grabbing up American cash to travel or just to hoard? You know, as a safeguard."

He shrugged.

"You think we'll stay? Or leave?" I asked. "I wish we knew."

"The church people wouldn't understand if we left. They'd think we're running away from a little discomfort."

"Exactly. It's just not possible to talk to them about this. Even before all this happened they never believed that Medellín was a violent place. And try to tell them the media calls Medellín the most violent city on earth! Forget it. They always say, 'I'm sure it's like this all over the world.' Most of them are NOT going to understand any particular danger for us as foreigners. They're just too used to living with violence."

"I met George at the bank. Their mission is sending them to Quito, Ecuador."

"Oh, flying?"

"Other missions feel highways aren't safe anymore."

I nodded.

"I would still go with the jeep," Harold said. "I don't rule out the highways yet."

"You mean we'd drive down to Cali? With the children?"

"Not Cali. People say Cali is going to be the next Medellín. The drug lords are strong there, too."

"This uncertainty is getting to me," I said. "I just feel totally disoriented. See that stack of newsletters on the buffet? Well, I should have sent them off today, but what do I write? I try to write one line, then it seems unsafe, too much disclosure. So, I write nothing. You think it's true that foreigners' mail will be checked? Some missionaries say our phones will be tapped."

"Too extreme. Nothing really serious has happened to foreigners yet. People get too dramatic."

"The whole darn situation is dramatic!" I said. "All the people talking about missiles and food shortages make me nervous! I wish a decision was made. Anything but this sitting around wondering."

The decision, though, was up to us. The mission boards of other denominations dictated from North America what their people should do, but ours said we'd know best since we were right on the ground. Earlier that year John Savoia, the team leader of our Colombian mission team, had retired back to the States. The Mission Board had asked Harold to be the next team leader. He had accepted on one condition—that he and I would be joint team leaders.

Now I wished I had none of the responsibility. We hoped for consensus of the whole team, of course. That was the Mennonite way of making decisions. But Harold and I would still have to answer for whatever decision was made.

The indecision was hard on our nerves. Harold and I were alternating between being greatest friends and snapping at each other. There were too many unknowns. What if we stayed and then the airport closed? Should I have bought so much food? What if we suddenly had to leave? Should I think of packing up, plan what to take, just in case? We had to prepare to leave and prepare to stay, both at the same time.

When I heard the school *buseta* around four o'clock I ran to unlock the front door. The children came bouncing into the house, happy and safe. I hugged them and sent them to wash up before having their snack.

Once they were seated around the table, I asked, "How was the ride home?" I wanted to fish for details, wanted to know if any dangers lurked along the way. But I didn't want to specify just what those dangers might be, not wanting to alarm the kids.

"Good," answered Conrad. "I didn't get sick."

"The bus driver gave us candy," Becky reported.

"Joey stuck his head out of the window and yelled stuff at people in English," Andy said.

"Oh no!" I said, horrified. Were all these foreign blonde kids taking The War as a joke? "That's awful. Didn't anyone tell him to stop?"

The kids shrugged. They were not concerned.

I wondered how much longer it would be safe to send a busload of fair-haired kids across the city each day.

46   Stay or leave?

Thursday evening, August 31. I was tucking Andy and Conrad into bed when the phone rang. Harold took the call. When I came downstairs, he told me quietly, "The school phoned."

"They did?"

"Yeah, no school tomorrow. All the Canadian Baptists including the teachers are holding a meeting. About whether they'll leave and where they'll go."

"They are?" I cried. "They'd close the school?"

He nodded.

"So, what happens to us then?"

"It's too dangerous to keep holding school out there on that finca anyway. They'd have to do something."

This was Harold talking? My risk-taker?

I wandered sadly into the living room. What should we do now? What would become of us and of the work we had been doing here and the people we worked with?

The Wesleyan workers were packing up, returning to the States. The Covenant families had been ordered to fly to Ecuador to await further orders and possible re-assignment elsewhere. And now the biggest group—the Baptists—were going to leave.

Should I start to pack? But what? Just clothes, I guess, or some valuables, too. Maybe a separate trunk could be packed with the computer and small appliances to be shipped later just in case we didn't return.

Harold went up to Matthew's bedroom to give him the news. I looked in on Becky and found her pulling back the covers to crawl into bed. I sat down on the edge of the bed.

"Becky, Mr. Rempel just called. There's no school tomorrow. Instead, the teachers and the other Baptist missionaries are going to have a meeting to decide what to do."

"Are they going to leave?"

"We don't know yet." Oh, if only I could reassure her. The children loved their school and would miss their friends terribly. Friends whose parents would also be planning where to take them to safety. They may never see their friends again.

"You know what would be good?" I said. "We might have to leave on short notice without much time to pack. So, it would be good if you'd look around your room and see what is really precious to you. Then you'll know what you want to take with you."

"Can I take Mitzi?"

I was pretty sure we wouldn't be taking Mitzi if we evacuated by plane. But she was so close to that little dog. They were inseparable now every hour she was home.

"We don't know yet, sweetheart," I said softly.

But an hour later when I slipped into her room to find her asleep, I saw tear stains still on her cheeks.

Life was so unfair. Of course, I didn't expect life to be fair for me, an adult. But for the children, I wanted life to be fair.

After checking the little boys in their bunks, I sat down on the sofa with pen and paper. The drapes were pulled tight. Across the back of my neck from one shoulder to the other ran a band of tightness I had never felt before.

Maybe, if I wrote down our options and made them more concrete, maybe then I could handle this better, not be so tense. I divided a page into two columns. Stay. Leave.

Stay:
- Buy food
- Bank account? Cash cheque.
- Try to get more American dollars.
- How to get the kids' schoolbooks out of the locked-up school?

Leave:
- Power of attorney for car, house. Leave keys.
- Buy plane tickets.
- Decide what to pack.
- Pack.
- Get *permiso* papers to take our kids out of country. (Go to DAS.)

- Find someone to live in and guard the house and take care of the dog.
- Say goodbye to the church people.
- Organize an ad hoc system to run the church until we come back.

Then I went up to bed. Harold and the kids were asleep, even Matthew. I lay in bed but I couldn't sleep. The unnatural silence from the curfew hung in the air like a claustrophobic blanket.

Then gunshots again punctuated the silence. Bang! Bang! Bang! Then silence. Complete silence. I imagined ugly scenes.

Maybe a warm cocoa would settle me. I got up and gingerly crossed the room in the dark. All the floors had what I called "cockroach floors." These were polished concrete tiles in an off-white colour splashed with black marks about the size of large cockroaches. I could never understand why these tiles were so popular in Medellín homes where everyone would want to recognize cockroaches to avoid stepping on them. In the dim light, the tile floor looked littered with the creatures.

In the kitchen I flicked on the light. Several surprised cockroaches exploring the counter tops scurried desperately to the nearest dark spot, some disappearing under the stovetop burners. I put on a small metal pot of milk to heat, hoping no cockroach would jump out at me. The sight of those long ugly creatures waving their antennae gave me goose bumps, what the Colombians called chicken skin.

In the living room I switched on the corner lamp and settled on the sofa with a mug in hand. I felt very alone and opened my Bible at a random spot, looking for comfort. A red and white slip of paper fell to my lap. I turned it over. On the back I saw my dad's handwriting.

The outdoor laundry area. See the black-spotted tile used throughout the house.

Then I remembered that on our last evening of furlough, together in my parents' home in Winnipeg, Dad had jotted down some Bible references and given the paper to me.

"Here," he said. "These are good ones."

Dad had a tradition he followed whenever one of the family left on a trip. He would gather everyone in the living room, open his well-thumbed Bible and read Psalm 121, the traveller's Psalm. Then he prayed for safe travels. Was it only two weeks ago that we sat around my parents' living room in Winnipeg listening to him read and pray?

Tonight, Canada was a whole world away. I missed the lakes, the open prairies, the quiet tree-lined shores and, on the west coast, the pounding of the surf we had enjoyed that summer.

I picked up the scrap of paper and my eyes misted at seeing my dad's familiar scrawl. He had jotted down four references, two from the Psalms. I looked those up first.

In Psalm 91, I read, "I've given my angels charge over you, to protect you."

Yes, Dad, that *is* good!

And even more specific was Psalm 27. "Even though a whole army surrounds me, I will not be afraid."

I leaned back on the sofa and closed my eyes. I let those words sink in deep behind my eyes and pour down over my soul. Then I let out a long sigh.

How had my dad known?

He was born in Russia in 1918, the same year as Solzhenitsyn. But, unlike that famous writer, my dad had not suffered under Stalin. When he was seven years old, his parents secretly fled the country and emigrated to Canada. Later, as an adult, he left a prosperous farming community in British Columbia to work as a missionary at an outpost in Manitoba. Later, working in the inner-city he met all kinds of people at the rescue centres and I remember him inviting ex-cons to our family Christmas celebrations. To be a risk-taker seemed normal to him.

He faced life with the same approach that Solzhenitsyn had put into words, albeit written in a context of incomparable danger, *If one is forever cautious, can one remain a human being?*

There on the sofa I thanked God for my parents, for Canada, for safety till now. Then I asked God for safety for the children and for wisdom to know what to do next.

I finally stood up and headed to bed. But before going up the stairs I opened the door of the pantry to peek at the rice and dried beans piled up there. I saw a stack of neatly packaged cubes of dried guava fruit, a lunchbox favourite. But if there was no school, there'd be no lunch boxes.

Well, if we were holed up at least we'd have fruit along with the carbs and protein. It struck me that all the foods I had chosen were typically Colombian. I was finally "at home" in this culture.

 ## 47   The phone rings

Friday, September 1. There were many phone calls during the morning, incoming and outgoing. School was shut down. The Baptists were leaving Medellín.

There was other major news too. The Canadian Prime Minister, Brian Mulroney, had now announced that he, too, along with the

American government, would support the extradition of drug lords. Now there was no more advantage to being Canadian. Escobar would be out to get us.

Peter and Eva, Galen and Linda came to our house to consult. With the school closed, the kids were home so we sent them to play in their rooms so they wouldn't hear our discussion.

"Now the narcos will be out to kill us Canadians as well."

"Yeah, and the school is run by Canadians so I wonder—"

"Oh no—they're pulling out. They called this morning. Teachers have to leave."

"For sure? It's definite?"

"School's shut down. That's it. Closed up."

"Darn! We can't even get the kids' books out or anything."

"And what'll we do for school for our kids?"

"Well," Peter said, "you should leave if the school's shut. But I wouldn't want to do anything like leave the country all together. That would mean all sorts of complications with visas and so on if once you were out and this thing prolonged itself."

"If only we knew for how long," I said. "It's so radical to just leave."

"Just go to Bogotá?" Harold suggested.

"Bogotá," Peter agreed. It's where we have others from our team. And that's the easiest place to leave from if you have to get out of the country. The airport's accessible."

"And the embassies are there," said Linda.

"Embassies, hah!" Eva piped up. "That might help you Americans. If *you* get stuck a plane flies in and gets you out. The Canadian policy is, *Here's some advice and now you're on your own.*"

It was agreed that because we had four children, our family also would leave the next day, Saturday, together with Galen and Linda and their three children. We would fly to Bogotá. Temporarily. The war was sure to end soon. We had never yet been to Bogotá so we would rely on our co-workers there to find temporary housing for us.

It was Friday noon. Twenty-four hours to get ready.

The plan was to hire a *buseta* to pick up Galen and Linda's family first and then to come by our house. Together we would ride to the airport. Everyone wondered, *Would that be safe?* But no one could think of a better alternative. We had not been able to gather enough cash for six airfares, so Peter lent us American dollars.

By evening the children had each amassed a little pile of possessions by their beds to take with them. Andy looked disconsolate. "I just put my posters up. What if there's another bomb and they get cut up?"

"We won't be away all that long, my dear," I said, stroking his hair. "And since they already bombed our house, they probably won't bother."

Conrad ate his night snack of cookies and milk at the dining room table. "I don't want to go in another airplane," he muttered. "I get sick in planes."

"This will be a short ride," I tried to cheer him. "You can take your teddy bear."

Conrad was silent a long time, staring into space. "Why is there a war, mom?"

I tried to explain for a five-year-old, but have no idea now what I told him. He thought about my answer, and then he looked at the upright piano across the room. Matthew had been playing piano for more than an hour but now was up in his room trying to fit a thousand books into his backpack.

"Our piano's going to be bombed up," Conrad announced.

"Oh, no, no. I don't think so."

"Well, it could be," he countered. "It sure could be."

Becky stayed all evening in her room with Mitzi. I had finally broken the news that Mitzi could not come. The little dog would stay back with whoever would be guarding our house.

At church, a prayer meeting had been previously scheduled for this Friday evening. Then, because of the curfew, it was changed to a *vigilia*, an all-night vigil since no one could go home anyway until the curfew lifted at six in the morning.

And now, given our sudden plan to leave Medellín, Harold drove to the Salvador barrio alone to break the news to our church people. I stayed home to pack and get the house ready to leave for a house sitter. I pictured Harold at the *vigilia* and I could imagine old Magda and Elida on their knees on the concrete floor, earnestly begging God to stop the violence. I pictured Guillo leading the group in vibrant choruses and hymns, plump Silvia raising her hands to heaven, Mariela closing her eyes to better shut out the world and sense the Holy Spirit.

Oh, I would miss these dear people. But surely, we would be back here soon again.

I said bedtime prayers with the children. Andy and Conrad prayed, "Help the school to open soon..." and "Help us find a good place to stay..."

Becky prayed, "Please make the bombs stop soon so we can come back home."

Matthew was still sorting through books in his room. He asked, "What kind of teacher will I have there?" He was already feeling the loss of Mr. McMonagle who had become his hero, the first teacher to fully respond to Matthew's thirst for learning.

I wished I could answer but I had no idea of what lay ahead.

Downstairs, I took a hot chocolate to the living room. I needed to think. During the afternoon Harold and I had called both our parents and the Mission office to tell them our plans.

"Aren't you coming home?" asked both sets of parents.

Home. There was that word again. Did I want to go "home"? Yes, I yearned for a home like Odysseus on his never-ending voyage. But unlike Odysseus, I did not know where that home was. Was Canada still home? We had wonderful friends there. But maybe we had changed too much to fit in with our old friends and our old life.

For Andy and Conrad, Canada was certainly not home. Andrew had a faint memory of snow and sleds but Conrad had never seen snow. For the kids, Colombia was home. That fact had sunk in that summer when, just before our furlough I had announced, "I'm so looking forward to taking a bath in Canada in a real bathtub!"

"Mom, what's a bathtub?" Conrad had asked.

Another time Harold announced that on furlough we would get to stay overnight in a cabin in the mountains.

"Dad, what's a cabin?" Conrad had asked.

Now tomorrow we were off to yet another city. We would land in Bogotá, an unknown place even to Harold and me, and another unfamiliar place for our children. My mind went searching for comfort. I remembered as a little girl falling asleep in the back seat of the car on the way home from a trip. What a delicious feeling when Dad picked me up and, all drowsy, I was placed into my bed and the covers pulled over. Where would I be tucking the kids into bed tomorrow?

48   Not the hockey bags!

Saturday, September 2. Harold came home from the *vigilia* around 6:30 in the morning. So weary. He had said goodbye to the church people on behalf of all of us. I was eager to hear how our Colombians had responded to the news but there was little time for anything but getting ready to leave.

I talked on the phone with Elsa whom I had looked to as a mentor. Her voice was sad. She knew that most foreigners had already left the city and so I was relieved that she was understanding. She blessed us to leave.

The children stuffed their treasures into backpacks while I tried to convince them that underwear and clean socks should take up more of the space than toys.

"And it's cool there," I told the kids, "so wear your jacket or sweater. Don't pack it away."

I sighed as I reached under the bed to haul out two blue canvas hockey bags. I thought I could still detect in them a faint odour of Canada. Just two weeks ago I had rolled them up and tucked them away under the bed, confident we wouldn't use them for another three years.

"We don't need those!" Harold exclaimed.

"Well, actually," I said, "the missionaries in Bogotá called. They don't have enough bedding for us all. We have to take sleeping bags and pillows."

There was a lot to do before the little *buseta* would come to carry us away.

I looked at the two large paintings on the *sala* wall. They were original watercolours by Mena, a Colombian artist. We had bought the canvases directly from Mena in Cali. One was of ships in the harbour at Cartagena and the other was of a village scene on the road between Medellín and Cali.

Our hockey bags, trunks and assorted suitcases when first arriving in Colombia.

I took one down and examined the back of it. We had had them professionally framed with sage green mats and gold-leaf frames. Brown paper covered the back.

"Let's take out these paintings, roll them up and put them in one of those big cardboard tubes," I said. "Then in case we do have to go back to Canada, they can be mailed to us."

I went to get a sharp knife. I came back and took hold of a frame.

No, I thought, *that's bizarre. I can't go around stripping paintings from their frames. That's just too radical.*

I hung it back on the wall. I said, "You know, I'm sure we'll be back in a few weeks. It's better to leave everything the way it is."

The *buseta* came before noon. We piled in our bags and I was glad Matthew was old enough to help with the luggage.

I looked back at our house. The tall lone palm tree beside the front door looked lonelier than ever. And all that glass that had been replaced after the bomb. It seemed we'd only looked through the windows a few times since.

Galen and Linda and their three children were already on the bus. They called out a cheerful, "Good morning!" I smiled. You'd think we were off on a picnic. I loved their spirit. Our children happily wriggled into seats and we all started asking each other what each had packed to take along.

But the Colombian driver looked solemn, understanding perfectly what was going on. Feeling heavy, probably, at the responsibility of getting this load of foreigners to the airport safely.

"Hey, did you remember everyone's documents?" Galen asked. He had reason to ask, remembering how we had scrambled to get that special letter for the kids the night before leaving on furlough. Each of us needed three documents: Colombian identity card, passport and visa. We had no plane tickets. We would just need to buy them at the airport and hope to get on a flight soon.

Our *buseta* lurched along through the crowded streets. Life looked like a normal Saturday in Medellín. Shopkeepers had their railings rolled up for business, sidewalks buzzed with hurrying people. All along the streets other buses screeched to a stop to pick up passengers. As we climbed the mountain toward the airport, we adults fell silent and the children talked in subdued voices.

From the bus's loudspeakers floated Colombia's salsa music. So familiar. I gazed out the window. Small roadside stands offered my favorite corn cakes, *arepas de choclo*. Would I see this city again or was this goodbye?

We breathed in relief when we pulled up at the José Maria Córdova Airport. But the airport had changed from when we had landed there two weeks ago. Now it was locked up tight. The only entrance was through one single narrow door. Only passengers could enter the airport, no one else.

Right inside the door stood a long table. A team of uniformed attendants were lined up behind it. We laid our bags down and each was opened and carefully hand-searched. Meanwhile, each one of us was briskly frisked before being allowed to actually enter the airport.

Instead of the usual bustling atmosphere, a vacant and eerie feeling hung over the beautiful interior under the glass dome. Two weeks ago, a busy thoroughfare where groups chattered and pushed their way through the crowds. Now, wide empty corridors. The few people we saw stared at us and our fair-haired children. They knew we were leaving and why. No one smiled.

In line to buy tickets for the next flight to Bogotá, I overheard the conversation between two Colombian women ahead of us.

"Have you heard? The offices of *El Espectador* were bombed this morning."

"In Bogotá?"

"Yes, of course Bogotá. Where they print the newspaper."

"You mean today?"

"Yes. This very morning, early."

"*Dios mío!* Why are we going to Bogotá? It's crazy. But there haven't been bombs there yet in the capital city."

"Well, it started there now. After all, it's a war."

I shook my head.

Dios mío indeed! Was Bogotá not a refuge after all?

Our bags were searched again by hand before we boarded. As our plane lifted off, I felt for Harold's hand. It was warm, comforting and real.

The rest of the scenario around me was unreal. Stuff like this happened to other people, not to me. Other people evacuated, not us. Yet here we were, evacuating the city.

But not the country. That was a blessing, I felt.

I counted my blessings. Our four children were with us. We were all healthy and well. We had caring families and friends praying for us back home.

If we had known what awaited us in Bogotá, would Harold and I have taken a different route? Chosen another path?

We thought we were leaving Escobar and the drug war behind us. But he would haunt us for the next seven years.

I never dreamt then that I would host former guerrilla fighters at our table.

Or that a bomb would again damage the house we lived in. When I was there.

Or that we would secretly support an air traffic controller who was under death threats from the drug lords.

I peered out the window of the plane. I couldn't see them but I knew our guardian angels flew alongside to protect us. We each had one. But to cover Harold, my risk-taker, there must be two. Or, maybe a whole committee.

And we'd need those angels in the days ahead.

Coming soon, the sequel: Seven Years in Bogotá

Acknowledgements

Thank you, Trevor McMonagle, for your excellent editing of the manuscript. I still fiddled a bit on the final copy, so any errors are my own.

Thank you, Wally Schmidt, for helping with the many photos.

Thank you, dear Harold, for making my writing studio come first, before other rooms, when doing the house renovations.

And thank you for filling my life with adventure!